NorthParadePublishing

©2012 North Parade Publishing Ltd.
4 North Parade,
Bath BA1 1LF. UK
Printed in China.
www.nppbooks.co.uk

Encyclopedia of Transport

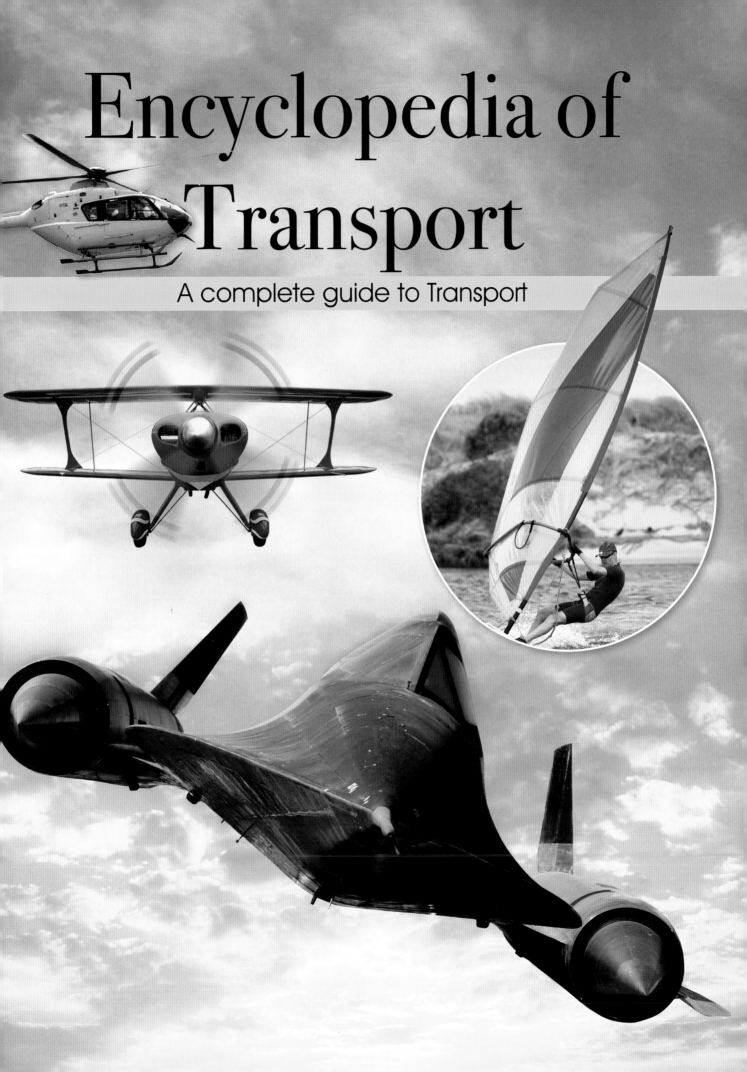

A complete guide to Transport

CONTENTS

AIRCRAFT

CARS

SHIPS AND BOATS

TRAINS

FLYING FIRSTS

From fabled Chinese princes and their flying chariots, to the mythical flying carpets of Persia, history and legend are full of tales about people who tried to reach up to the skies. Indeed, one of man's earliest dreams was to fly!

▶ *Sir Geroge Cayley*

Early Birds

In 1670, an Italian monk, in his attempt to create a balloon, designed a strange machine – four airfilled spheres attached to a boat! The first successful balloon was flown only a century later, by the Montgolfier Brothers.

Various other ideas for lightweight balloons and flying machines followed, but it was Sir George Cayley, an Englishman, who changed the course of flight history. Starting with motor gliders, Cayley built all kinds of machines to test his ideas for making heavier-than-air objects fly. He was the first man to study the scientific principles of flight.

Flying High

The first successful aeroplane was the Wright Brothers' Flyer of 1903. It was made of cloth and paper. Today, aeroplanes, helicopters, gliders and other lightweight aircraft have made travelling around the world not only possible, but easy too!

▲ *A present day model of The Montgolfier Balloon in flight*

Who launched the first hot-air balloon?

In November 1783, Etienne and Joseph Montgolfier, wealthy paper merchants, launched the first hot-air balloon. Pieces of straw and bits of wool were burnt as fuel to sustain the flight.

Which was the first air crash to be recorded on camera?

The *Hindenberg*, a huge German zeppelin, burst into flames while landing in New Jersey, U.S., in 1937. The tragedy was taped by press reporters present at the airport.

When was the first commercial air service established?

In 1910, Count Ferdinand von Zeppelin of Germany started the first commercial air service between Europe and America. The airships were called "zeppelins".

Why did George Cayley's Aerial Carriage never take off?

The Aerial Carriage could not be tested because George Cayley could not find the right engine for it! The 1843 convertiplane combined the concepts of an aeroplane and a helicopter, and had four rotors resembling the wheels of a carriage.

▼ *The Hindenburg*

What was the inspiration behind Sir George Cayley's glider?

An ordinary kite inspired Sir George Cayley to invent the glider. His first glider had a movable tail and was mounted on wooden sticks.

What was special about the 1913 *Sikorsky Bolshoi* airliner?

The *Sikorsky Bolshoi* airliner of 1913 was the first four-engine aircraft to fly. Besides being the largest aircraft at the time, it was also the first to have a large passenger cabin.

Who made the first successful flight across the English Channel?

French pilot Louis Bleriot made the first flight across the English Channel in 1909. The flight won Bleriot a prize of 1,000 pounds. The aircraft used by him came to be known as *Cross-Channel Bleriot XI*.

◄ *George Cayley's vertical flight mechanism*

FACT BOX

● Harriet Quimby was the first licensed female pilot in America. In 1912, she also became the first woman to fly across the English Channel.

● In 1924, two Douglas World Cruisers (DWC), taking off from Seattle, Washington, made the first around-the-world flight. The expedition was completed in 175 days.

● Sir George Cayley, known as the "Father of Aerial Navigation", was the first to think about vertical flight (elevation). In 1799, he designed the first aeroplane with wings, a fuselage, a tail unit and a mechanism that made vertical flight possible.

▲ *Sir George Cayley's Aerial Carriage*

▲ The 1903 Flyer was made of natural materials like spruce and ash

How did the French inventor Besnier experiment with flying?

Besnier first attached four huge panels on to levers, which he rested on his shoulders. In imitation of a bird in flight, he moved the levers with his hands and feet, reaching the ground safely from the top of a house!

Who was the first woman to fly a supersonic plane?

In 1953, Jacqueline Cochran, an American pilot, became the first woman to fly faster than the speed of sound (supersonic speed). At the time of her death in 1980, she held more speed, altitude and distance records than any other pilot in history.

Who was the first woman to fly solo across the Atlantic?

American aviator Amelia Earhart flew solo across the Atlantic in 1932. In 1937 she set out for an around-the-world flight. However, more than halfway into her journey, her plane mysteriously vanished.

Which was the world's first jet airliner to enter regular passenger service?

The *De Havilland Comet* - flying from London to Johannesburg on May 2, 1952 - was the world's first jet airliner to enter regular passenger service.

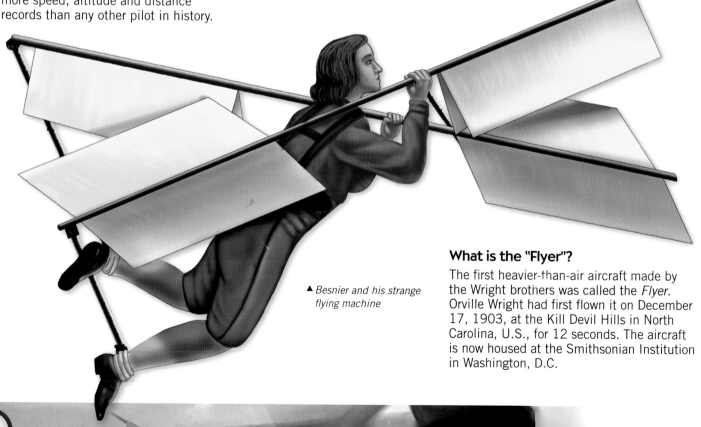

▲ Besnier and his strange flying machine

What is the "Flyer"?

The first heavier-than-air aircraft made by the Wright brothers was called the *Flyer*. Orville Wright had first flown it on December 17, 1903, at the Kill Devil Hills in North Carolina, U.S., for 12 seconds. The aircraft is now housed at the Smithsonian Institution in Washington, D.C.

TYPES OF AIRCRAFT

The dream of flying spurred people to invent many different forms of air machines.

At First...
Gliders were the first aircraft with wings. Airships were very popular in the early 1900's.

Hovering Helicopters
Helicopters benefit over other aircraft for their ability to move in all directions. They can even hover in mid-air! The first successful helicopter dates back to 1936.

Unlimited Uses
Passenger liners and private jets carry millions across the world every day. Air forces have extremely sophisticated aircraft to protect their nations. Other aircraft include cargo planes, seaplanes, supersonic jets and even flying cars! There are smaller, lighter and easy-to-fly aircraft that many people fly for fun.

◀ *The microlight is a lightweight plane developed in the 1970's from hang-gliders*

FACT BOX

- Lightweight aircraft with small engines are called ultralights. They are usually home-built, inexpensive and easy to fly.

- The Boeing Company is one of the world's biggest manufacturers of commercial aircraft. The American company delivers hundreds of new aircraft every year.

- The Boeing 747, or the "jumbo jet", was for many years the world's largest passenger aeroplane. The first prototype of this large aircraft was rolled out in 1968. Powered with a jet engine, the plane can carry over 400 passengers.

▼ The Boeing 747 passenger liner

What is the difference between a biplane and a triplane?
Triplanes have three wings, one above the other, while biplanes only have two. The extra wing gives triplanes greater moving and lifting power. These were used as fighter planes during World War I (1914-18).

What is a monoplane?
A narrow aeroplane with a single set of supporting wings is called a monoplane. Louis Bleriot's *Cross-Channel Bleriot XI* was a monoplane. Most modern aeroplanes are monoplanes too.

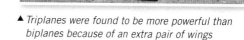

▼ *The first aeroplane to fly was a biplane*

▲ *Triplanes were found to be more powerful than biplanes because of an extra pair of wings*

How do cargo planes carry goods from one place to another?

Cargo aeroplanes are designed to transport all types of goods, such as parcels, military weapons, animals, vehicles and even other small aircraft. These goods are usually stored in the sides of the plane. Some planes, like the Boeing 747-400, have noses that can open up for storing large cargo.

Why was Moulton Taylor's aircraft design unique?

Moulton Taylor, an American inventor, designed the Aerocar, an aeroplane that can also be converted into a car! The change could be performed in about 15 minutes, with the wings being folded back along its sides.

▲ *A cargo plane*

Why were biplanes considered better than monoplanes?

Unlike monoplanes, biplanes have two sets of wings, one placed above the other and supported by wires. In the early 20th century, the biplane was considered stronger than the monoplane.

What is the difference between the terms "aircraft" and "aeroplane"?

The term "aircraft" refers to all flying machines, including aeroplanes, helicopters and hot-air balloons. Aircraft may range from simple hang-gliders to the enormous jumbo jets. The "aeroplane", on the other hand, is a powered, heavier-than-air aircraft with fixed wings.

◄ *Taylor's Aerocar*

What are airships commonly used for?

The earliest use of airships was to carry people from one place to another. This helium-filled aircraft was soon replaced with more sophisticated aeroplanes for passenger service. Airships are now mainly unmanned and used for advertising or taking aerial photographs.

What is the function of observation planes?

Observation planes are usually standard light aircraft. These are used by the police or the army for investigation purposes. Rescue services also use observation planes to locate victims after a mishap, or to study the location of the mishap.

Are all jet aircraft supersonic?

Supersonic planes are only those jet aircraft that can travel faster than the speed of sound. Their shape is different from that of conventional aeroplanes. They also require large quantities of fuel to sustain their high-powered flight.

Why are tiltrotor aeroplanes so called?

A tiltrotor plane's engines and propellers tilt in different directions to fly. The rotors are tilted upward for vertical flight, and forward for fast, forward movement.

Are there any aeroplanes that can land on water?

Seaplanes can take off from, as well as land on, water. They do not need a runway like other aeroplanes. These planes are largely used by defence forces to strengthen their marine attack. They are also used in remote areas such as northern Canada and Alaska, which have few airfields.

What advantages do propellered planes have over jet aircraft?

Propellered planes have propellers that are driven by gas turbines. As a result, these planes are cheaper to run than jet aircraft. They can also take off easily from short runways. However, these planes are unsuitable for travelling long distances.

▲ *Tiltrotors combine the best functional features of aeroplanes and helicopters*

WAR CRY!

Fighter planes, bombers, spy planes and observation aircraft play a crucial role in warfare.

Not a Smooth Start, but....

In September 1908, in order to test the famous Flyer, American Lieutenant Thomas Selfridge went on a flight with Orville Wright. Unfortunately, the propeller broke and the plane crashed. However, it were the Wright Brothers who, in 1909, finally built the world's first military aeroplane.

▲ The Sopwith Pup was the first British fighter designed to fire through the propeller

The World Wars

The World Wars greatly changed the way military planes were used. From being merely tools for observation, they were modified for use in bombing and air attacks. Dutchman Anthony Fokker designed a system for firing a machine gun through an aircraft's propeller. The British BE2 was one of the first aircraft to drop bombs.

▼ The Stealth Bomber is protected by its shape

With World War II came the era of jet-propelled aircraft, and faster, more powerful warplanes. The fabric-covered biplanes were replaced by metal-bodied monoplanes.

What are fighter planes used for?

The fastest of all warplanes, fighters are designed to win air superiority so that other slower aircraft, like observers and bombers, can operate over battle zones. Fighters carry out ground attacks as well as assaults on enemy fighter planes. The Russian MiG-25 is one of the fastest fighter aircraft in service.

Which country owns the Northrop B-2 Stealth Bomber?

The United States owns the Northrop B-2 Stealth Bomber. This warplane is designed to absorb or deflect enemy radar, so that it can remain undetected while approaching its targets.

What role do aircraft usually play in warfare?

There are a variety of aircraft specially designed for war. They are equipped with sophisticated electronic instruments. Their role in war ranges from detecting and attacking enemy targets, to supplying weapons to other aircraft. Some aircraft are also used for carrying troops from one battle zone to another.

▲ A bomber plane

What kinds of weapons do fighter planes use to attack enemy aircraft?

Fighter planes use a variety of fire missiles, torpedoes, machine guns and bombs to fire at enemies. One such weapon is the air-to-air AIM-9 Sidewinder missile. It is classified as a smart weapon because it has an in-built system that allows it to home in on its target.

What are weapon-carrying warplanes known as?

Bombers are used for carrying weapons and bombs during a war. They have even been used to carry nuclear weapons. Some bombers are equipped with special bombs that can destroy runways on enemy airfields.

How effective are helicopters as war aircraft?

Helicopters are used to move troops and equipment rapidly into battle zones. Heavily armed helicopters called helicopter gunships are widely used during war. These are equipped with rapid-fire machine guns that fire from the turret.

Are there special planes for observing and reporting the movement of enemy forces?

Aerial Reconnaissance Planes, or observation planes, are airborne observers that report the movement of enemy forces. These planes are a prime target for enemy fighters. Observation planes are usually pilotless and remote-controlled.

How do wings help fighter planes to fly faster and evade enemy attack in the air?

Some military aeroplanes, like the F-14 Tomcat fighter, are equipped with "swing wings". These wings are fully spread out during take-off, but, once in the air, they can fully swing to the back of the aircraft. This not only helps the aeroplane to fly faster, but also allows it to dodge low-flying enemy aircraft.

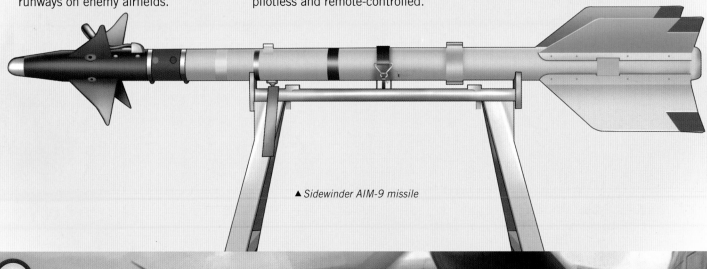

▲ Sidewinder AIM-9 missile

◄ The "swing wings" of the F-14 Tomcat fighter make the plane flexible

FACT BOX

- The *US F22 Raptor* is said to be the world's most expensive fighter aircraft. Built by Lockheed Martin Aeronautical Systems in the 1990's, it cost over $150 million to develop!

- V/STOL (Vertical/Short Take-Off and Landing) aircraft use very short runways, or no runway at all. The power of their jet engines allows them to rise vertically, or just after a short run.

- The *Black Widow* is the world's smallest spy aircraft - it can fit into the palm of an adult hand! It can stay airborne for 30 minutes and carries a camera that sends pictures to a special pair of glasses worn by its operator!

How many people are needed to crew a fighter plane?

The term "aircrew" includes the flight crew and the ground crew. A fighter plane usually carries a two member crew - the pilot and the weapon-systems operator. The pilot carries flight plans in his knee pads.

What kind of a warplane is the Harrier?

British Aerospace's Harrier, or "jump jet", is a V/STOL aircraft. It can fly in all directions and can even hover like a helicopter. Its wheels fold up into the wings during flight. The "jump jet" is a very useful warplane because it can take off or land almost anywhere.

How can the flight crew of an aircraft escape in the face of a probable crash?

Most military aircraft have ejector seats that shoot the crew out to safety. In an emergency, the crew members pull a handle that releases the cockpit canopy. They are then shot out of the aircraft along with their seats. Once the crew member falls to a particular height, the seat automatically falls away and a parachute opens up.

Which fighter aeroplane was the first to set records for speed, climbing speed and height?

The F-104 (Starfighter) was the first fighter aeroplane to set world records for speed, ascending speed and height. The aircraft is built with a short wingspan, making it lightweight. In fact, the F-104 Starfighter is so light, it is sometimes called the "missle with a man in it!"

▼ The F-104 (Starfighter)

▲ V/STOL aircraft

THE METALLIC BIRD

The earliest experiments in flying were not very successful. These were done with airfilled bags and hand-movable flaps, which were good enough only for a short stay in mid-air. The early inventors did not fully understand the basic science of flying.

Aerodynamics

Aerodynamics is the study of air in motion. The name originated from the Greek words "aer", meaning air, and "dynamis", which means power. It is this science that makes it possible for aircraft to fly. Aerodynamics observes the forces that act on solid objects moving in air, and how the air acts upon an aircraft's aerofoil (wing).

Four Forces

There are four forces that act on an aeroplane in flight - lift, weight, thrust and drag. Weight refers to the force of gravity on the aircraft. Lift is the upward force that balances the aircraft's weight. Thrust is the forward push of the aircraft. Drag is the force of air that slows down forward movement.

▲ An aeroplane can fly only when its lift is greater than its weight, and when the thrust of its engines is greater than the drag of the air

Elevator

Fusel

Ailerons to steer the plane

Flap

Why do aeroplanes have a streamlined body?

Streamlining cuts down drag, or air resistance, by helping air to flow smoothly past an object. Teardrop shaped objects such as aerofoils are streamlined for this reason. The lesser the drag, the better the movement of the aeroplane.

What does the term "airframe" stand for?

The fuselage (the central body portion), wings, tailplane and tailfin are together called the airframe of an aeroplane. These make up the main structural features of an aeroplane. While the fuselage lends weight to the aircraft, the wings carry it into air and the tail keeps it steady.

What made the *Flyer* a success despite its not having a streamlined body?

The *Flyer* was a biplane that did not have a streamlined body. However, drag increases only with speed, and the *Flyer* did not fly fast enough to make streamlining necessary.

How do aerofoils affect the airflow around an aeroplane?

The upper surface of an aerofoil is longer - and more curved - than its lower surface. The air flowing over the aerofoil has to travel farther than the air below. In order to keep up with the speed of the air flowing below, the air above the aerofoil ends up travelling faster. This helps to create lift.

How do the flaps and slats on aeroplane wings work?

Aeroplane wings are equipped with flaps and slats for achieving extra lift. By extending the size of the wings and the curve of the aerofoils, they spread out the airflow over a larger area. These features also facilitate swift take-offs and slow, smooth landings. Flaps are located on the trailing edges of the wings, while slats are situated on the leading edges of the engine.

How heavy are the wings of an aeroplane?

An aeroplane's wings are not solid, but hollow. A thin skin of lightweight material covers the aerofoil structure supported by the girder-shaped wing beam. This makes the wings strong, but as light as possible.

How do swing wings contribute to an aeroplane's speed and lift?

During take-off and landing, moveable swing wings are stretched out for good lift. During flight, however, these are swept back in order to reduce drag and increase speed. Modern jets like Panavia Tornado Adv, 1984, have moveable swing wings.

FACT BOX

- Propellers, or airscrews, are fan-like objects fixed either on the aeroplane's nose, or on the wings. As a propeller turns, its blades pull in air from the front and push it out the back.

- The pointed nose of the Concorde helped the aeroplane fly at great speed. However, during take-offs and landings, the nose blocked the pilot's view; hence, the nose had an instrument that allowed it to "droop" down, away from the pilot's view!

- Gliders have special air brakes on their wings that help the aircraft descend quickly and smoothly for landing.

▼ *Propellers are driven by the aeroplane's engine. They thrust the aeroplane forwards just as the wings lift it upwards*

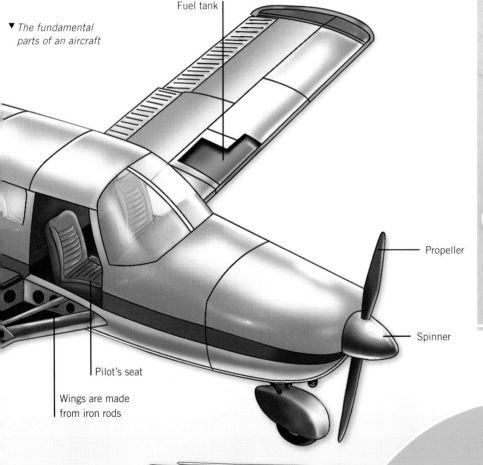

▼ *The fundamental parts of an aircraft*

Fuel tank

Propeller

Spinner

Pilot's seat

Wings are made from iron rods

Slats

Flaps

▶ *Aeroplane wings have slats and flaps that help in flight. Flaps increase the wing size, which gives the aircraft more lift for take-off. Slats help to reduce lift before an aircraft lands*

Why are aeroplane tyres filled with nitrogen gas?

Aeroplane tyres are filled with nitrogen because it is incombustible, i.e. it does not burn. During take-offs and landings, the tyres can rub the ground so hard that they may generate enough heat to catch fire.

What is the role of the aeroplane's rudder?

The rudder of an aeroplane helps to steer the plane in flight. It is situated in the tail section.

Why do most aeroplanes require a runway almost 1,500m (4,921 ft) long?

Winged aircraft can fly only when there is enough lift to overcome their weight. Lift is the upward force that pushes aircraft into air. It is created when air pressure over the wings decreases. Air pressure, in turn, decreases with speed. Aeroplanes move along the runway to keep air flowing past their wings, with the flow much faster above than below. This helps create the required lift.

▼ The jet engine of an aeroplane

Why do some warplanes have retractable main wheels?

Some warplanes, like the Supermarine Spitfire of 1936, have wheels that can be pulled up during flight. As the wheels are pulled out of the airflow, drag is reduced and speed increases. The Supermarine Spitfire became famous as a combat machine during World War II.

What kind of engines do the fastest aeroplanes have?

The fastest aeroplanes are equipped with jet engines. These engines suck air in at one end and force it out of the other at a much greater speed. This action thrusts the aircraft in the opposite direction. The engine burns fuel and pushes exhaust gases out from the back at enormous speed. This backward push thrusts the aeroplane forward quickly.

◄ The front gear tyre of an aeroplane

FLYING AN AEROPLANE

Each part of an aeroplane – the fuselage, wings, undercarriage (landing gear) and tail assembly – is vital to flight. The airframe of an aeroplane refers to the basic plane.

Tail Talk

A very important feature of an aeroplane is the tail assembly. It is the stabilising force that controls the aircraft's swing. It is also used to control any pitching and yawing.

The tail assembly is made up of a horizontal stabiliser and elevators, and a vertical fin and rudder. The stabiliser keeps the aircraft steady during flight, and prevents the plane's nose from swinging sideways (yawing). The tail also safeguards the nose against up-and-down movements (pitching).

Tail Types

The tail assembly comes in an array of designs, each useful for different kinds of movements. Some common ones include: right-angle assembly, swept-back assembly, T-assembly, Anhedral assembly, V-assembly and twin assembly. The V-assembly, also known as the Butterfly, is preferred for lighter planes. Most jet engines, on the other hand, use the T-assembly.

▼ The tail assembly of an aeroplane is also called empennage

FACT BOX

- An aeroplane's yoke moves the plane in the same way as a steering wheel moves a car. When the yoke is pulled back, the plane moves up; if pushed forward, the plane goes down.

- Lincoln Beachey, regarded as the "father of aerobatic flying", became the first American, in 1913, to perform the "loop-the-loop" stunt in his aeroplane Curtiss.

- Aeroplanes often bump up and down in flight. This is known as turbulence, and is caused by the layers of atmospheric air constantly moving up and down. Just as boats bounce along the ocean's waves, aeroplanes, too, ride the layers of air in the sky.

What are control surfaces?

All aeroplanes have moveable parts on their wings and tail. The moveable parts on the wings are the ailerons, and those on the tail are the elevators and the rudder. Together, they are known as control surfaces. They are used to change the direction of the flow of air, so that the aeroplane can turn or tilt in flight.

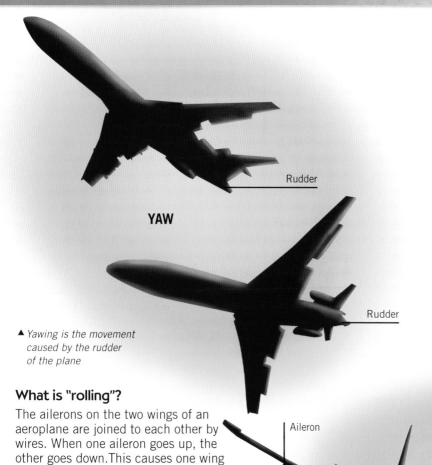

YAW

Rudder

Rudder

▲ *Yawing is the movement caused by the rudder of the plane*

What are the main kinds of movements made by an aeroplane in flight?

The main movements made by an aeroplane in flight are rolling, pitching and yawing. Moving the rudder in a specific direction turns the nose of the aeroplane in that direction. This helps the aeroplane take a turn while flying.'

Do passenger airliners need multiple engines?

Passenger airliners show great variety in the number and position of their engines. While some airliners have four engines (two mounted on each wing), others have three engines distributed between their wings and the tail. All airliners are designed in such a way that they are able to land safely on just one engine, should the others fail.

What is "rolling"?

The ailerons on the two wings of an aeroplane are joined to each other by wires. When one aileron goes up, the other goes down.This causes one wing to rise and the other to drop, making the aircraft tilt to one side. This change of position of the aeroplane is called "rolling" (or "banking").

What is "pitching"?

The action of elevators on the movement of an aeroplane is called "pitching".When the elevators are raised, the nose of the plane points upwards and its tail dips down. Thus, the aeroplane is said to be pitched upwards as it gains altitude after take-off.

Aileron

ROLL

Aileron

▲ *The rolling movement of an aircraft*

▼ *The elevators of an aeroplane cause pitching*

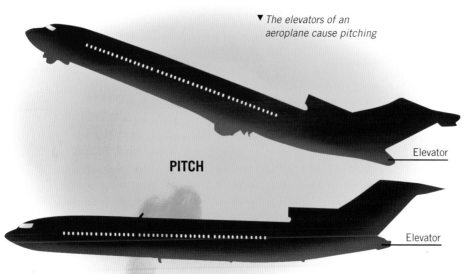

PITCH

Elevator

Elevator

How are the control surfaces operated to turn or tilt the aeroplane?

In most aeroplanes, the control surfaces are moved hydraulically - i.e., through the pressure exerted by an oily fluid pumped along pipes. In modern "fly-by-wire" aircraft, such as the Airbus A320, complex computer systems operate the controls. In the earliest models, however, the control surfaces had to be physically monitored by the pilot.

Is it possible for an aeroplane to fly upside down?

An aeroplane can be flown upside down and this is called inverted flight. Aerobatic planes are specially used to perform all kinds of aerial stunts like rolling and looping.

◄ Ernst Mach

What is a sonic boom?

When an aircraft flies faster than sound, the air in front of it gets compressed and forms a shock wave. The aircraft breaks through the shock wave, which reaches your ears as a loud bang. This loud bang is known as a sonic boom.

How are the cabin lights and air conditioning of a grounded plane powered?

A small engine called the auxiliary power unit (APU) is used when the aeroplane is grounded and the main engines are switched off. The APU drives electrical generators to supply power for cabin lights and air conditioning as passengers board or get off the plane.

What is the Mach number of an aircraft?

The Mach number for an aircraft is the measurement of its speed in terms of the speed of sound. It is named after the Austrian scientist, Ernest Mach, who worked it out. The number is calculated by dividing the aircraft's speed by the speed of sound. Thus, Mach 1 is the speed of sound (1,060 kph) and Mach 2 is twice the speed of sound.

What type of engines do gliders use?

Gliders are non-powered aircraft and have no engines. They are pulled, or towed, attaining gradual speed and lift. Either an aeroplane or a car tows the glider until the latter gets enough lift to glide in the air on its own!

What flight controls does a pilot use to fly an aeroplane?

A pilot flies their aeroplane by using various flight controls. These include the control stick, a pair of rudder pedals and a throttle lever. The throttle lever controls the engine power.

▶ The throttle levers of an aeroplane

FINDING THE WAY

In the 1920's, as aeroplanes began to carry more and more people across longer distances, it became essential to set up air traffic systems to control and guide aircraft.

Radios and Radars

By the end of World War II, there were radio and radar networks capable of tracking many aircraft at a time. Radars reflect aircraft positions on display screens. Controllers can warn pilots of possible collisions with other aircraft.

Light the Way

Earlier, aircraft did not fly very high, and could be directed by hand signals. In the late 1930's, controllers started using light guns that sent out coloured light beams to aircraft. This system worked well for night flights too.

Safety in the Skies

Today, air traffic control is a vital part of all modern-day airports. Controllers keep track of all aircraft, from the time they taxi onto the runway, to the take-off and landing stages.

▲ Earlier, flags were waved to guide aircraft. Green-coloured flags meant pilots could go ahead with take-off or landing. Red flags directed pilots to wait for further instructions

How does air traffic control (ATC) help in ensuring a safe flight?

In the area around and above an airport, each aircraft is guided by the ATC. Air traffic controllers speak to flight captains by radio. Information about each aircraft's height and position is collected by radar antennae at the airport and displayed on screens in the control tower. The controllers maintain a close watch on the path taken by the aircraft.

Do pilots plan the details of a flight before they take off?

Before a take-off, the captain of a flight must file a "flight plan" with the air traffic control (ATC). The flight plan shows details of the route that the aeroplane will follow, along with the height and the speed at which it will fly. No aeroplane can take off without the approval of the flight plan by the ATC.

How do pilots on a flight know if they are keeping to their flight plan?

Ground-based radio transmitters, or radio beacons, emit radio signals that are caught by the radio system on an aeroplane. Pilots use the beacons as signposts to help them keep to their flight plan.

What is an air corridor?

An air corridor is a narrow, strip-like route that an aeroplane must fly along. Each aeroplane is assigned its own invisible air corridor by the air traffic control. No two aeroplanes have a common air corridor at a time. This keeps them away from each other and prevents mid-air collisions.

Can aeroplanes land without informing the air traffic control at the airport?

At the end of a flight, the flight captain radios the ATC to ask for permission to land. The controllers guide the aircrew to bring the aeroplane down safely. The engine power is reduced so that the aeroplane loses speed and height as it nears
the runway.

How far apart are air corridors from one another?

Although air corridors criss-cross at certain places, there is a safe minimum distance that must be maintained between two aircraft. There must also be a minimum time gap between the take-off and landing of commercial flights.

How do radar systems work?

A radar system works by sending out short bursts of radio signals. Like echoes, these signals bounce off any object they hit. The computers fitted in the aeroplane's flight deck record the time taken by the signals to bounce back and then calculate the distance between the object and the aircraft. This information is then displayed on a screen on the flight deck.

▲ *Devices on-board the aircraft keep traffic control towers informed of its whereabouts at all times*

▲ *Radar signals*

◀ *All airports have radar systems to keep track of aircraft*

FACT BOX

- A pre-flight weather inspection informs pilots about imminent thunderstorms. Graphs, maps and radar reports show where and when storms are likely to occur. A weather radar device on-board the aeroplane can detect water, so the crew is forewarned about bad weather.

- Radar stands for "radio detection and ranging". Most planes have radar equipment in their nose cones. It cautions pilots about bad weather and objects they may fly into.

- Earlier, pilots used to find their way by looking out of the window for landmarks. Sometimes they even used automobile road maps! In 1919, Lieutenant Bruner, an American, started using bonfires to navigate planes at night.

What role do lighting systems play in flight safety?

Lighting systems are required both for night and day flights. All runways have lights positioned along the sides and down the middle. Rotating beacons on the top of control towers act like road traffic signals. Red-coloured obstruction warning lights are also provided to warn pilots of any danger ahead.

How are aircraft guided after landing?

After landing, the taxiing aircraft are guided by ground movement controllers to their parking positions in the hangar.

▲ *Obstruction warning lights*

◄ *Ground traffic controller*

How do air traffic controllers keep track of aircraft movements?

Air traffic controllers keep track of moving aeroplanes through radarscopes. Devices inside an aeroplane send signals to the radar reciever. These signals are then displayed on the radarscope. The tiny dots on the screen represent the aeroplanes in flight.

How do pilots find their way high up in the clouds without being able to see the ground?

Pilots and air traffic controllers use electronic systems to help them navigate. These systems transmit information beamed from radio equipment on the aeroplane, on the ground, and on satellites orbiting high above the earth.

Why do aeroplanes wait at the runway before take-off?

When an aeroplane is ready to leave, the captain radios the control tower for permission to start the engines. The aeroplane then taxies on to the runway, getting the engines to build up enough power to take-off.

AIRCRAFT TECHNOLOGY

Before the invention of powered flight, flying machines lacked engine power. In the 1920's, the unusual *Ca 60* was built with nine wings and eight engines! It crashed on its very first flight, soon after take-off.

Engine Count

Today, there are single-engine, twin-engine, three-engine and four-engine aircraft. Most modern aeroplanes have three or four engines. Single-engine aircraft are generally preferred for pilot training.

Body Basics

The first flying machines were made of paper, linen, straw and other natural materials. Since then, aircraft technology has advanced tremendously. Now we have aircraft made of metal (like aluminium) and alloy (like steel). Those with non-metallic bodies - made of materials like Kevlar and carbon fibre - are much lighter and, often, much stronger too.

The Boeing 777 was the first aeroplane to be designed entirely on computer. Some three million different parts were put together using 3D computer graphics!

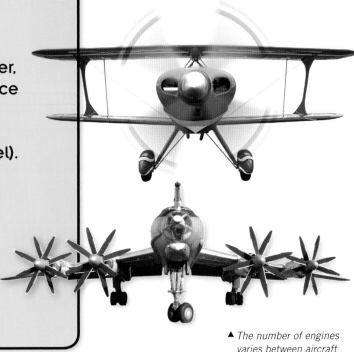

▲ *The number of engines varies between aircraft*

Is it possible for aircraft to be refuelled during flight?

Aircraft tanks can be refuelled even while they are airborne. This is called air-to-air refuelling. A tanker aircraft extends a long hose, or a pole, to the aircraft it has to refuel. The refuelling pilot then aligns the plane so that its tank connects with the end of the hose or pole.

Can computers fly aeroplanes on their own?

The autopilot is a computer device that can fly an aeroplane on its own. It is mostly used on long flights. However, a pilot is always present in the cockpit to keep an eye on the autopilot, to ensure the flight is going according to plan.

How do pilots know the height at which they are flying the aircraft?

The cockpit has an instrument called the altimeter, which shows the height (above sea level) at which the aircraft is flying. It does so by measuring the air pressure outside the aircraft. Air pressure decreases with height; so the lower the air pressure, the higher is the aircraft.

▼ Refuelling an aeroplane in mid-air

What is the electronic altitude director indicator (EADI)?

The EADI is a flight instrument that tells the pilot whether the aeroplane is flying at the correct level. It is a round dial indicating the angle at which the aeroplane is flying. There are small lines, or bars, for depicting the position of the aeroplane with respect to the ground and the horizon.

Who was Charles Edward Taylor ?

Charles Edward Taylor (1869-1956) was the world's first aeroplane mechanic. Taylor took about six weeks to build the engine for the *Wright Flyer*.

How are autopilots used on short flights?

Autopilots play a limited but important role on short flights. Besides helping the pilot to fly the aeroplane, they also run frequent checks during the flight to ensure that all the systems are working properly.

▼ *The black box helps to investigate what went wrong in an accident*

FLIGHT RECORDER DO NOT OPEN

Do aeroplanes have speed indicators?

The air speed indicator (ASI) in the cockpit shows the speed in terms of knots (1 knot = 1.85 kph) and the Mach number. Information about the aeroplane's speed through the air is fed to the ASI from a sensor called the pitot tube, fitted outside the aircraft.

▼ *The cockpit of an aeroplane*

FACT BOX

- The first person to fly an aircraft at supersonic speed was Charles Yeager. In October 1947, the World War II pilot broke the sound barrier with the *Bell X-1*.

- The autopilot was invented by Lawrence Sperry. He also invented other flight instruments, as well as the aerial torpedo weapon and the parachute pack that pilots use in emergencies.

- Aeroplanes are fitted with a fire-and-crash-proof flight data recorder. This recorder, called the black box, is usually red in colour and records everything that happens to the aircraft's main systems. It even records the conversations between members of the flight crew.

Is a flight engineer part of an aeroplane's flight crew?

Flight engineers used to be part of the flight crew in the past (the first known onboard flight engineer was Charley Furnas). Most modern airliners have a two-member crew, comprising of the captain (pilot) and the co-pilot. The systems that were earlier managed by the flight engineer are now monitored by electronic equipment.

How do flight simulators recreate the runway, the clouds and other scenery outside the aircraft?

Scenes from real airports are projected on to a screen outside the cockpit window. This lets pilots practice take-offs and landings in "real" conditions. For a more realistic effect, aircraft sounds are fed through loudspeakers inside the simulator.

▶ *A vital member of the aircrew: the pilot*

What are flight simulators?

Flight simulators are machines used for training pilots to fly new types of aircraft and to practice flying skills, including what to do in an emergency. These machines look like giant computer games. They cost millions of pounds to develop but are vital in ensuring the safety of the training process.

Do flight simulators use electronic equipment similar to that in the cockpit of an aeroplane?

A flight simulator has the same flight deck as an aeroplane, complete with all the electronic controls. While trainee pilots manage the controls, an instructor sits behind them at all times for guidance. There are different simulators for different types of aeroplanes.

How do pilots experience the tilting and turning of an aeroplane while sitting in a flight simulator?

A flight simulator has legs that move to tilt in all directions. While the simulator is actually fixed to the ground, it is capable of tilting. This feature lets the pilot inside feel as though he is actually flying through air.

27

ON A FLIGHT

Passengers of modern air travel are treated to all kinds of on-board comforts - movies, music, telephone and email facilities, shopping, interesting menus, personal attention and spacious seats.

Aircraft Attendants

Flight attendants did not appear until the late 1920's, when some airliners hired male assistants. Called flight companions, cabin boys, or stewards, they attended to luggage and helped nervous passengers relax.

In 1930, Boeing introduced the first female flight attendants. They served passengers with sandwiches and water, besides chewing gum to help ease popping ears!

The Jet Age

The advent of commercial jets brought about higher standards of technology and comfort. Trained ground staff and aircrew were introduced. In the mid-1930's, Douglas planes came with soundproof cabins, upholstered seats and padded armrests.

Passengers can now choose from the different classes of comfort offered by almost every airline.

▲ Nowadays, sleeper seats with personal TVs and headphones provide home-like comfort to passengers

When did a telephone service first feature in-flight?

In 1984, Airfone launched the world's first in-flight telephone system. The service was introduced on American Airlines aircraft. Today, most new aircraft have in-flight telephone services.

How are the life jackets on-board an aircraft helpful in an emergency?

Each passenger seat has a life jacket tucked under it. During emergency landings at sea, passengers wear these life jackets before coming out of the aircraft. Once outside, they pull the toggle on the jackets to fill them with air. The air-filled jackets keep the passengers afloat on water.

How do escape chutes help in transporting passengers to safety?

Escape chutes are slide-like, inclined ramps made of lightweight material. In case of emergency landings, chutes are inflated at the exit doors. Passengers slide down the chutes to the ground. At sea, they may be folded and used as life rafts.

▶ An air hostess explains how to use life jackets

Why are oxygen masks kept in the passenger cabin of an airliner?

Air pressure decreases with height above ground level. The air in the passenger cabin is artificially pressurised to maintain the same air pressure as that on the ground. If, however, the cabin air pressure falls, oxygen masks drop down to allow people to breathe safely.

Who proposed the inclusion of nurses in a flight crew?

In 1930, Ellen Church, a nurse, suggested that nurses be included in a flight crew for attending to sick passengers. Boeing then promptly hired eight nurses for its crew. However, it is no longer compulsory for flight attendants to have a degree in nursing.

Which airline was the first to hire a fashion designer for flight attendant uniforms?

In 1965, Braniff Airlines hired fashion stylist Emilio Pucci to design uniforms for its flight attendants. The American airline was also the first to train women in airline mechanics.

Which was the first airline to serve freshly brewed coffee on a flight?

Trans World Airlines was the first to serve freshly brewed coffee on-board a flight. The New York-based airlines is also believed to be the first to have introduced a special section for non-smokers.

Who was the world's first air-crash victim?

On September 17, 1908, Thomas Selfridge became the world's first air-crash victim as the Wright Model A crashed at Fort Myer, Virginia. Selfridge was a passenger on the plane, which was being piloted by Orville Wright. While Orville survived the crash, Selfridge died on the spot.

Has the Concorde ever had a major accident?

The Concorde, the fastest passenger aeroplane in the world, faced its first major accident nearly 30 years after its first flight. On July 25, 2000, an Air France Concorde crashed shortly after take-off. It was suspected that a thin metal strip blew one of its tyres, which in turn ruptured the fuel tanks, causing the crash. All the 109 people on-board were killed.

Which airline company was the first to introduce a range of menus to choose from?

Virgin Atlantic was the first airline to offer a choice of meals on-board. It was also the first to place video screens in the back of every seat in every one of its aircraft.

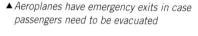

▲ Aeroplanes have emergency exits in case passengers need to be evacuated

FACT BOX

● In the 1930's, the Boeing 314 Clippers were designed to include over 30 sleeping cabins, a dining room, a lounge, a bar, dressing rooms and even bridal suites!

● The first toilet in an aeroplane is believed to have been designed by pioneer Igor Sikorsky in 1913, on-board the *Russky Vityaz*.

● The first in-flight meal was served in 1919, on a flight from London to Paris. The meal was said to include cream teas and cooked game. Food served during flight is kept cool on trolleys with dry ice. This helps to keep the food fresh.

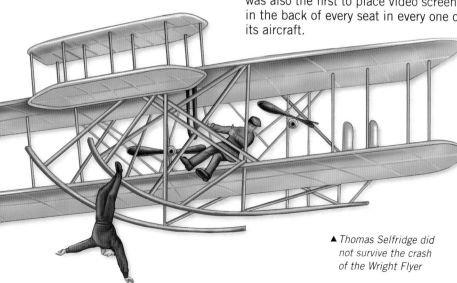

▲ Thomas Selfridge did not survive the crash of the Wright Flyer

SHAPES IN THE SKY

From balloons and airships to modern aeroplanes, there have been many experiments in aircraft design. How has the shape and design of aircraft changed over time?

Strange Shapes!

The earliest flying machines were strange to look at. The first successful airship, built in 1852, was shaped like a cigar. Later, Leonard Bonney made a seagull-like aeroplane.

The unusual shape of the Lockheed F-114A keeps it from detection by enemy radars. Popularly called the Stealth Fighter, it was designed in the 1970's. More recently, in 1984, the Rutan Voyager was built in an H-shaped design.

Science of Shapes

Aircraft design is based on aerodynamics. The shape of the fuselage can reduce drag and weight, or increase lift and thrust. Today, computers help people design aircraft in the most favourable shapes.

However, an efficient and safe design is useless unless it is practicable. For instance, passenger airliners like the Boeing 747 also have to be spacious, with room for passengers and cargo.

▼ The Rutan Voyager was the first to make a non-stop flight around the world without being refuelled

▼ Special aircraft are designed to carry out crop-dusting

Which is the world's largest international airport?

King Fahd International Airport, located near Dammam, Saudi Arabia, is the largest in the world in terms of area, covering 301 sq/miles (780 sq/km)! This makes it slightly larger than the neighbouring country of Bahrain.

Where was aerial crop dusting first carried out?

Crop-dusting - the process of spraying fertilizer, insecticide or fungicide (in powdered form) on crops from an aircraft - was first carried out in Ohio, U.S., in 1921. Lt. John B. Macready sprayed some insecticide from a Curtiss JN-6 light aircraft in order to treat an insect-infested grove.

▶ Leonardo da Vinci's sketch of a flying machine

Which famous painter studied the flight of birds and sketched the basic design of an aeroplane?

Leonardo da Vinci (1452-1519), the great Italian artist known for his masterpiece Mona Lisa, was one of the first people to investigate flight. He was so fascinated with the idea that he sketched plans for all sorts of flying machines. He studied the flight of bats and birds, and came up with designs for an ornithopter, or flapping-wing aircraft.

What is the Codex Hammer?

The Codex Hammer is one of the notebooks of Leonardo da Vinci containing his scientific drawings. In 1994, it was acquired by the American billionaire, Bill Gates (owner of Microsoft), for $30,800,000 in an auction at Christie's in New York.

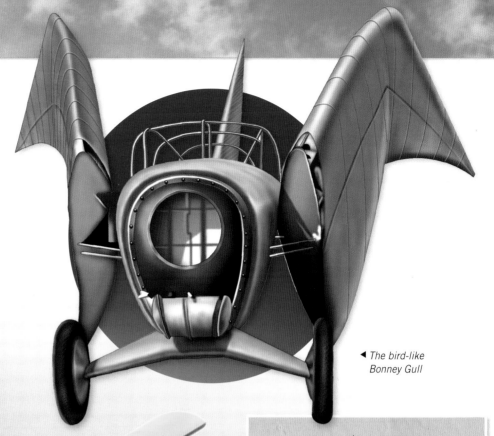

◄ *The bird-like Bonney Gull*

Who built an aeroplane named Bonney Gull?

In the 1920's, Leonard Bonney built an aeroplane that he named *Bonney Gull*. He named it so because he had modelled it on seagulls!

What was the profession of Orville and Wilbur Wright before they began designing aircraft and became famous?

The Wright brothers were bicycle mechanics before they began designing aircraft. Their first successful glider went on some 1,000 flights. Later, they built the *Flyer*, the earliest heavier-than-air, powered aircraft. Orville Wright took the Flyer on its first, 12 second long flight in 1903.

Which is the fastest aircraft in the world?

The North American X-15 is the fastest aircraft in the world. In 1967, it reached a speed of Mach 6.72, which is over six times the speed of sound. The X-15 does not have a jet engine. It is powered by a rocket.

FACT BOX

● Icarus, the son of Daedalus, attached wax wings to his body and flew a little too close to the sun. His wings melted and he fell to his death in the sea. This legend is said to be about 2,000 years old and has become a symbol of impractical ambition.

● The Wright Brothers' *Vin Fiz* was the first aircraft to cross the North American continent. It was also the first to have an advertising message on it. Since the trip was being sponsored by the Armour Meat Packing Company, the plane carried a message for the company's grape drink below its wings!

● Tibet's Bangdag Airport, at about 4,300 metres (14,107 feet) above sea level, is the world's highest airport. It cost some $29.6 million to build.

Is aeroplane racing a recognised sport?

Aeroplane racing, although not as popular as car racing, is a recognised sport. Fat, short aeroplanes called Gee Bees take part in these races. Balloon races were very popular before the invention of the aeroplane. The world's first international balloon race was held in 1906 in France.

What is special about the Lockheed SR-71 Blackbird?

The Lockheed SR-71 Blackbird is the world's fastest aircraft driven by a jet engine. This U.S. spy aircraft touched Mach 3.3 in 1976. It is no longer in military service, but is now used for scientific research into the upper layers of the atmosphere.

What happened to the Concorde?

The Concorde, which could travel at more than twice the speed of sound, flew regular trans-Atlantic flight for 27 years until a high-profile crash, the aftermath of 9/11 and other factors led to the plane's retirement in 2003. Jointly developed by Britain and France, in retirement, Concorde remains an icon of aircraft history.

▼ The Concorde was one of the most distinctive flying machines ever made

What is the *Spruce Goose*?

The American flying boat, *Spruce Goose*, is the largest aircraft ever to have been built (in terms of wingspan). This 55m (181 ft) long boat was built in 1947 from laminated birch wood. It was piloted by an American millionaire, Howard Hughes, on its one and only flight. The Spruce Goose got its name after its huge size made it impossible to use! It is now a part of the Evergreen International Aviation Museum, Oregon.

How long did the first non-stop, around-the-world flight last?

The fist non-stop, around-the world flight lasted exactly 94 hours and 1 minute. Captain James Gallagher and his crew achieved the feat in the year 1948, in a Boeing B-50A Superfortress. Taking off from Fort Worth, Texas, the aircraft was refuelled four times in mid-flight.

◄ The Lockheed SR-71 Blackbird

HELICOPTER HIGHS

Among the many innovations in aircraft, the helicopter particularly stands out. Moving in ways that no aeroplane can, the helicopter is considered to be the most versatile flying machine.

The forces that work on an aeroplane – lift, weight, thrust and drag – also work on a helicopter. So what makes the helicopter more adaptable? What enables it to fly backwards and hover in the air without moving?

Copter Components

Helicopters come in many different types, but they all share certain basic features.

The most important component of a helicopter is the main rotor, or propeller. The propeller's blades, situated above the fuselage, provide the helicopter with lift as well as the means to move forward, backward and sideways. The helicopter usually has a tail boom jutting out at the back, at the end of which is the tail rotor. This keeps the helicopter from spinning around while the main rotor is still running. It also lets the pilot steer the helicopter through left and right directions.

▼ *A helicopter's rotors can continue rotating even after a power failure. As the helicopter descends, the force of air over the blades keeps the rotors propelling. This gives the helicopter enough lift to have a controlled landing*

▶ *A rescue helicopter*

Who was Louis Breguet?

Louis Breguet was a French designer who, in 1907, designed the first helicopter to be flown by a pilot. Breguet was airborne for one minute, while his helpers kept the helicopter in place with ropes, so that it would not fly away!

When was the first known flying helicopter invented?

The earliest known flying helicopter was built in 1784 by two Frenchmen, Launoy and Bienvenu. They fixed two rotors, made of turkey feathers, on the tips of a pole. A spring fixed between the rotors caused the rotors to propel for a few seconds, sending the "helicopter" spinning. The Frenchmen had based their design on the Chinese spinning top!

How are helicopters handy in emergencies?

For one, helicopters can avoid the traffic and attend to emergencies quicker than ambulances. The ability to hover in mid-air allows helicopters to rescue people by lowering stretchers or harnesses on to the ground. Some rescue helicopters even have equipment that helps locate people in the dark by their body heat!

FACT BOX

- The first president to use a helicopter was Dwight D. Eisenhower. The lawns of the White House served as a helipad. Eisenhower was also the first president to have a pilot's licence!

- The first female pilot to fly around the world in a helicopter was Jennifer Murray from England. The 57 year old flew a total distance of 35,698 miles (57,449 km) in a Robinson R44 Astro. The trip took 97 days.

- Igor Sikorsky is regarded as the "Father of Helicopters". Although he did not invent the very first helicopter, he built the first successful one, setting the standards for future designs.

▲ Helipads atop buildings are convenient for business people and VIPs who need to avoid the public

What was the duration of the first flight made by the VS-300 helicopter?

On its very first flight in 1941, the VS-300 set a world record for the time, by flying for 1 hour and 33 minutes.

Who built the "Flying Bicycle"?

In 1907, Paul Cornu, a French bicycle maker, invented a helicopter that had two rotors fixed on to bicycle-like wheels. It stayed in the air for about 20 seconds. To stop it from flying off in another direction, men on the ground are said to have held it in place with sticks!

Which was the first single-propeller helicopter?

The Sikorsky VS-300 was the world's first single-rotor helicopter. The aircraft was designed by Igor Sikorsky in 1940. Deployed during World War II by British and American forces, it also became the first helicopter to be used for military purposes.

What is a helipad?

A helipad is a landing place for a helicopter. It is quite common to find one at hospitals and office towers, since it helps patients and business professionals save time. Such helipads are usually located on the rooftops of buildings.

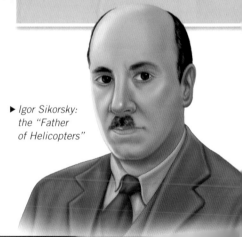

▶ Igor Sikorsky: the "Father of Helicopters"

What is unique about the CarterCopter?

The CarterCopter is a gyroplane that features both a rotor and a fixed wing. During take-off, the rotor provides the aircraft with lift, like in common helicopters. Once the CarterCopter gains height and speed, its fixed wing provides for a steady increase in lift, as is the case with fixed-wing aeroplanes. The CarterCopter's propeller is fully computerised and lightweight.

What can a helicopter do that an aeroplane cannot?

Unlike an aeroplane, the helicopter can fly backwards, hover in the air without moving, and even rotate in mid-air!

What does the word "helicopter" mean?

The word "helicopter" comes from the Greek terms - *helix*, which means "spiral", and *pteron*, meaning "wing".

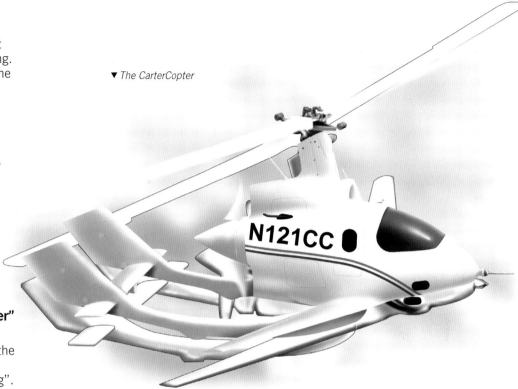

▼ *The CarterCopter*

N121CC

Why can't helicopters fly as fast as fixed wing aircraft?

There are many contributing factors: the main reasons are that the forward-moving rotor blade creates too much drag; also, in order for the helicopter to remain stable the rotors have to be flexible, which in turn combats the limits of lift and thrust that can be provided.

▶ *Aerial filming has become easier thanks to helicopters with in-built cameras and filming equipment*

What role do helicopters play in the world of television and cinema?

Helicopters are one of the most popular means of aerial filming. They are extensively used by television and cinema crews when shooting. Nowadays, aerial filming services are common all over the world. Hi-tech helicopters come ready with fixed cameras and other sophisticated filming gadgets.

CAR CRAZE

For as long as history records, people have been devising ways to move from one place to another. The first self-propelled vehicle (not drawn by animals) appeared in 1769, when Frenchman Nicholas Cugnot built a steam-powered carriage. It moved at only 5 km (3 miles) per hour.

The Motor Generation

The motor car came of age with the invention of the internal-combustion engine. Its development started in the 1850's. The first petrol-driven engine was perfected by Gottlieb Daimler around 1880. From the 1890's onwards, cars fitted with small steam engines were used in the United States.

Then, in 1908 came the Ford Model T – a landmark creation. It was the first car to be mass-produced, which made it available and affordable for ordinary people. Since then, the craze for cars has continued and the motor car remains a source of utmost fascination.

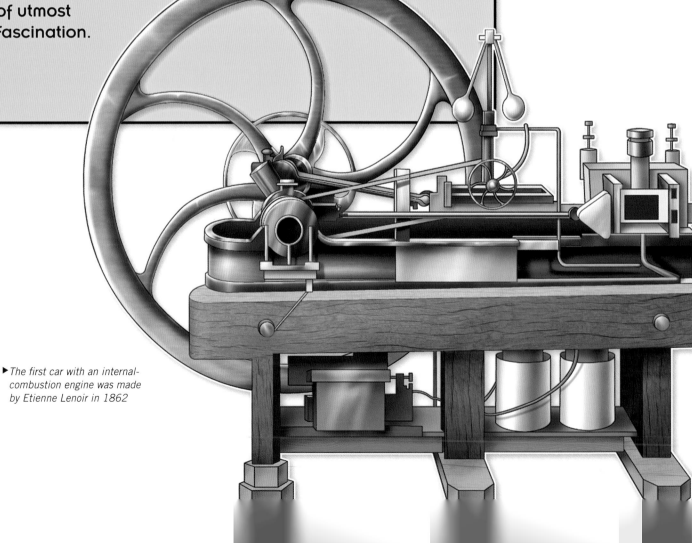

► The first car with an internal-combustion engine was made by Etienne Lenoir in 1862

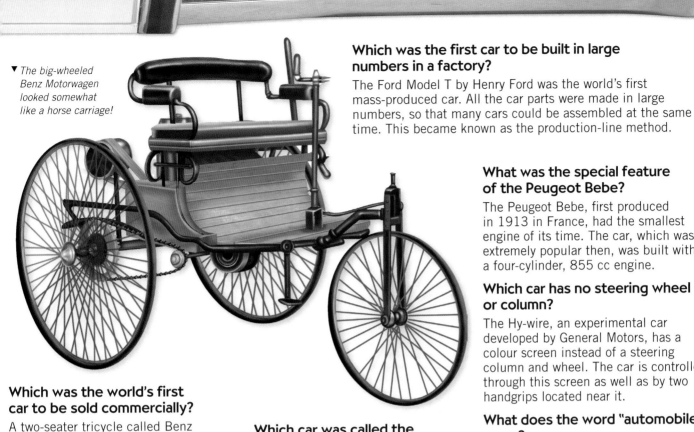

▼ The big-wheeled Benz Motorwagen looked somewhat like a horse carriage!

Which was the first car to be built in large numbers in a factory?

The Ford Model T by Henry Ford was the world's first mass-produced car. All the car parts were made in large numbers, so that many cars could be assembled at the same time. This became known as the production-line method.

What was the special feature of the Peugeot Bebe?

The Peugeot Bebe, first produced in 1913 in France, had the smallest engine of its time. The car, which was extremely popular then, was built with a four-cylinder, 855 cc engine.

Which car has no steering wheel or column?

The Hy-wire, an experimental car developed by General Motors, has a colour screen instead of a steering column and wheel. The car is controlled through this screen as well as by two handgrips located near it.

Which was the world's first car to be sold commercially?

A two-seater tricycle called Benz Motorwagen was the first commercial car. It was made in 1885 by Karl Benz, a carriage builder.

Were some cars in the 1950's run on motorcycle engines?

The German BMW Isetta, a microcar, was powered by a motorcycle engine. Microcars are nicknamed "Bubblecars" because of their round shape and large windows.

Which car was called the "Hummingbird"?

The earliest motorized London taxi was called the "Hummingbird". The 1897 Bersey electric car got its name because it made a humming sound.

How do modern factories make millions of cars in just a few days?

Modern factories use Ford's production-line method to manufacture cars. Some machines weld metal parts together, some attach fittings, and others spray paint.

What does the word "automobile" mean?

The word "automobile" is a combination of the Greek word "auto", which means "self", and the French word "mobile", which means "moving".

When was a petrol-run car first driven?

In 1870, Siegfried Marcus of Austria first drove a car on petrol. It was so noisy that Marcus was banned from driving it again.

▶ The Marcus car was the first to use gasoline as a fuel

Did early car drivers wear special clothing while driving?

Since early cars had no windscreens, drivers had to wear thick goggles to protect their eyes from stones and dust. They also wore woollen clothes to keep warm in open cars.

▲ Early drivers wore special goggles as protective gear

How long was the Morris Mini Minor?

The Morris Mini Minor, introduced in 1959, was a four-seater "family" car, but it had a length of only 304 cm (120 inches). One of the most popular cars of its time, it is still widely considered to be one of the best-designed compact cars.

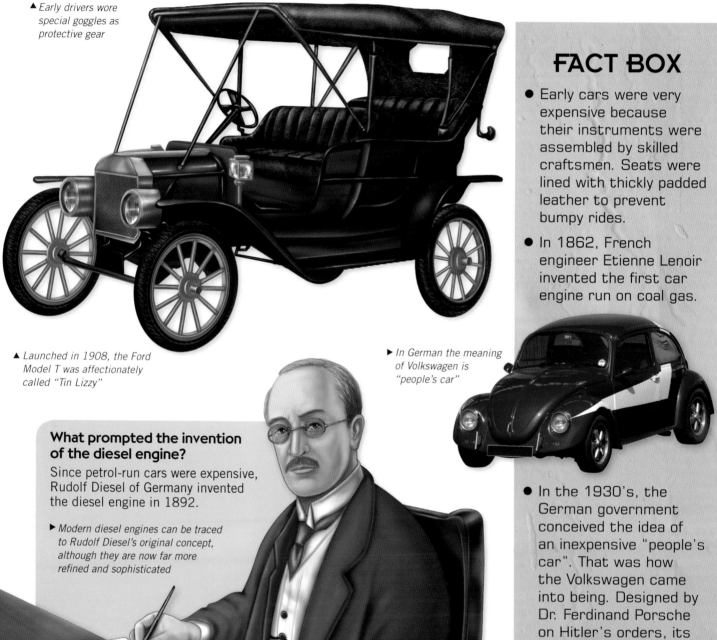

▲ Launched in 1908, the Ford Model T was affectionately called "Tin Lizzy"

FACT BOX

● Early cars were very expensive because their instruments were assembled by skilled craftsmen. Seats were lined with thickly padded leather to prevent bumpy rides.

● In 1862, French engineer Etienne Lenoir invented the first car engine run on coal gas.

▶ In German the meaning of Volkswagen is "people's car"

● In the 1930's, the German government conceived the idea of an inexpensive "people's car". That was how the Volkswagen came into being. Designed by Dr. Ferdinand Porsche on Hitler's orders, its unusual shape earned it the nickname "Beetle".

What prompted the invention of the diesel engine?

Since petrol-run cars were expensive, Rudolf Diesel of Germany invented the diesel engine in 1892.

▶ Modern diesel engines can be traced to Rudolf Diesel's original concept, although they are now far more refined and sophisticated

In the beginning, cars needed a lot of clearance space between the ground and the floor of the car in order to travel over bumpy and rutted roads, so they used large wheels. Modified from horse carts, the wheels used to be very heavy too. They were usually made of iron and wood. Today, wheels are manufactured from alloys or compressed steel. They are not only durable and strong, but lightweight and compact as well.

Comfy Wheels

An early type of tyre was made of solid rubber. In spite of giving a hard ride, without any cushioning effect, it never suffered from punctures and was therefore quite popular. Later, pneumatic (air-filled) tyres – offering a softer and more comfortable ride – were introduced. The first such tyres were very narrow, with an inner tube that had very high level of air pressure. Later still, a wider "balloon" tyre was developed. It had a lower level of air pressure and was less rigid than the first pneumatic tyres. The result was a smoother ride!

▲ This early, heavy wheel has iron spokes and a wooden rim

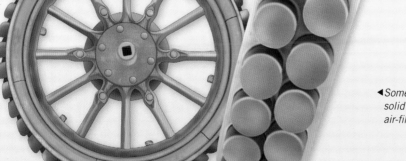

◄ Some early tyres were made of solid rubber, unlike the modern air-filled rubber tyre

▲ *Grooves increase the grip of a tyre and help prevent a car from skidding and sliding on the road*

Why do cars skid on wet roads?

As a car speeds down a wet road, water forms a film around the tyres. This can lift the tyres off the road surface, causing the car to skid. To prevent this, tyres have drain channels to push the water away from under the tyre as it rotates.

Who is the Michelin Man?

The Michelin Man is the well-known trademark of the Michelin tyre company of France. It features a "man" – made entirely out of tyres – juggling a ring of tyres over his head.

Why do tyres have an uneven surface?

Tyres have raised pads, small grooves and water draining channels on their surface so that they can grip the road well. A smooth tyre tends to skid as it moves.

Do all cars have the same type of tyres?

Different cars have different tyres depending on their size and shape, as well as the type of roads and weather conditions of a particular area. Thus, there are winter tyres for cool regions.

Why are tyres so important for a car's performance?

Tyres come in contact with many different types of road surfaces, such as rough, smooth, wet, dry and icy. Tyres are crucial to both safety and performance because if they do not grip the road securely and steadily, a car cannot stop, turn corners, or speed up efficiently.

Why are three-wheeled cars not popular?

Most modern cars are four-wheeled, with a wheel placed at each corner. This evenly distributes the car's weight on the road.

Are ordinary tyres suitable for racing cars?

Racing-car tyres are made of very hard rubber mixtures to cope with heat generated from the car's speed on a racetrack. Ordinary tyres would melt in such conditions. Sometimes, racing cars use smooth tyres ("slicks") to reduce friction and achieve extremely high speeds.

▶ *A bubble-shaped, three-wheeled car that did not remain popular for very long*

▼ *Racing cars use special tyres made of extremely tough rubber, as well as smooth "slick" tyres without grooves*

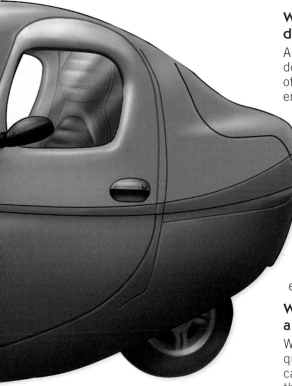

Why do tractors have high, deeply grooved tyres?

A tractor tyre's grooves are designed to grip the slippery mud of farms. The height of the tyre enables easy passage over obstacles, while the width spreads the weight of the tractor on the ground.

Why is "hydroplaning" dangerous?

Hydroplaning happens when a car is driven over so much water that all four tyres lose their grip on the road. The car gets lifted off the ground and remains supported only by water. This is dangerous because there is no traction and the car can easily go out of control.

What makes smoke appear from a car's wheels?

When a driver either accelerates quickly or brakes suddenly, the tyres can rub on the ground. This causes the rubber to burn with the heat of the friction, releasing smoke.

▼ *The grooves of a tractor tyre are especially deep, so that the vehicle does not slip and slide while moving over muddy terrain*

A CAR RIDE

There are many things that contribute to the look, feel and handling of a car. Automotive technology is now so advanced that cars are constantly being updated, modified and reinvented.

Honk! Honk!

One device that allows a car to make its presence felt is the horn! Early cars had a wide array of horns, such as air-bulb horns and "trumpet" horns. The Clarion Bell was a "hands-free" gong that could be operated by the driver's foot. It allowed the driver to use both his hands to control the car.

A Big Hand

Accessories are an important aspect of any car and this was true for early motorists as well. Before flashing indicators became a standard feature, there were some unusual gadgets that served the purpose of signalling. One such was a mechanical hand that was attached to the car door. The driver rotated a knob built into the dashboard in order to position the hand for various signals.

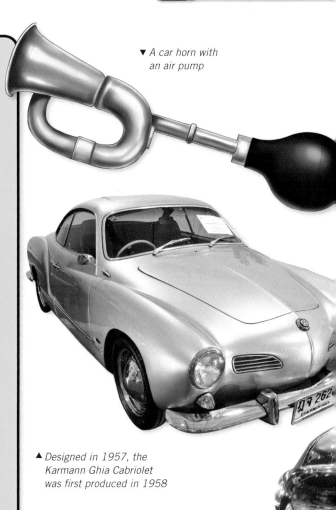

▼ A car horn with an air pump

▲ Designed in 1957, the Karmann Ghia Cabriolet was first produced in 1958

▼The Lamborghini Diablo is one of the most iconic supercars

Why does the Lamborghini Diablo have a 12-cylinder engine?

The Lamborghini Diablo is a very powerful car that needs a lot of energy to accelerate quickly. Its 12-cylinder engine burns much more fuel than an ordinary 4-cylinder car, thus helping it generate the required energy.

Why do cars have multiple gears?

Cars have several gears to achieve different combinations of speed and force. The first and second gears provide more force than speed. The fourth gear is used for driving on flat roads, while the fifth is for high speed. Cars may have up to six gears, depending on cost, use and design.

Why is it unsafe to drive a car with wet brakes?

Disc brakes function due to friction between brake pads. Since water reduces this friction, a driver may lose control of the vehicle if the brakes are wet.

What is a convertible?

A convertible is a car with a roof that can be folded back. The hood can be fixed over the car during winter, or when it rains.

What kind of horns did early cars have?

A rubber bulb attached to a brass tube – that was the horn for most early cars! When the driver squeezed the bulb, air travelled through the tube and made a sound as it came out the other end.

▼A super-luxury limousine provides the ultimate ride in terms of comfort and glamour

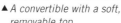

▲ A convertible with a soft, removable top

Are there any car brakes that are used only after the car is parked?

Parking brakes, operated by the handbrake lever, lock the rear wheels when the car is standing still.

What makes luxury cars, such as the limousine, bump-free?

Cars use suspension systems to prevent bumpy rides. Luxury cars like the limousine have the Selective Ride Control (SRC) Suspension System to provide an extra-smooth ride.

What are blue headlights?

Headlights that produce a bluish light are becoming popular because they produce more light and are also more energy efficient. These new blue headlights use a technology called high intensity discharge (HID).

Are there cars with wings?

A number of cars, including the Porsche 911 Turbo, have a wing attached to the rear. Known as a spoiler, it creates downforce, helping the car grip the road at higher speeds wheen cornering

FACT BOX

- Early cars had lamps on one side of their bonnets. These were lit by burning oil or gas. Oil was usually carried in a small container at the bottom of the lamp.

- In modern cars, windshield wipers are designed and manufactured to be operational for at least 1.5 million wipes.

- The first functional car radio was named Motorola because it was a kind of "moving radio" (radio in motion). Motorola went on to become a world-famous brand.

Racing cars symbolise sheer velocity, thrilling adventure and intense competition. These awesome speed machines now come in the latest ultra-light materials and some are so low-slung that they seem to be almost touching the ground. These features, along with extra wide wheels and hugely powerful engines, enable the cars to attain amazing speeds. Often termed as "aerodynamic", the sleek and streamlined bodies of racing cars help reduce the drag from the air rushing past the car.

Suction Skirt

Racing cars are designed to make use of air pressure. Initially, most of them had a kind of "skirt" that almost reached the ground. This created a vacuum beneath the speeding car which was filled by the surrounding air. The resultant "suction" effect helped keep the car firmly on the ground. "Skirts" were later banned because these encouraged drivers to race at extremely high – and risky – speeds.

On a Bend

Grand Prix circuits have sharp bends specifically to restrain excessive speeds that may lead to dangerous accidents. These are also a test of the drivers' skills.

▼A car racing around sharp bends is a thrilling sight!

When was the world's first long distance car race held?

The world's first long-distance car race was from Paris to Bordeaux in 1895. Emile Levassor won it in 48 hours but was later disqualified.

Are sports cars successful racing cars?

Sports cars, or roadsters, can be driven in races as well as on ordinary roads. Their bodies and engines are usually tested for toughness at the Le Mans 24 hour race in France. The Jaguar D Type won the Le Mans 24 hour race four times between 1953 and 1957.

What was special about Ferrari's F1-2000 engine?

The Ferrari F1-2000 with its V10 engine was a smaller, more compact, and more powerful version of the typical Ferrari engine. Michael Schumacher drove it to victory in October 2000.

What is the most popular kind of track racing?

Formula One racing, or Grand Prix, is the most popular kind of track racing. The first Grand Prix was held in France in 1904.

▶ The first Grand Prix car race held in 1904 included cars made by Mercedes, Fiat and Renault

▼ *The Ferrari F1-2000 weighed about 600 kg (1,323 pounds)*

When did Ferrari first win a world championship event?

Ferrari had its first-ever F1 victory when its driver, Froilan Gonzalez, won the R.A.C. British Grand Prix at Silverstone in 1951.

What are hairpin bends on a racetrack?

Sharp bends on racetracks are known as hairpin bends. As the cars speed towards the bend, drivers have to brake hard and then accelerate again after passing the bend, all at the very limit of the car's ability.

◄ *The chequered flag is said to have been first used in motor sport around 1913*

What is common between chess and car racing?

The black-and-white chequered pattern associated with a chessboard is also a symbol of motor racing. It is waved when cars cross the finishing line after a race.

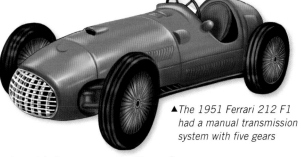

▲ *The 1951 Ferrari 212 F1 had a manual transmission system with five gears*

FACT BOX

- Rear-view mirrors were invented in the 1920's. Prior to this, a mechanic seated in the car used to warn the driver about another vehicle trying to overtake him.

◄ *The rear-view mirror made it unnecessary for a mechanic to sit with the driver and guide him*

In which car race is the winner awarded a quart glass bottle of chilled milk?

The winner of the Indianapolis 500 race is presented a quart glass bottle of chilled milk, along with a flower-studded wreath. Louis Meyer, the 1936 winner, started the tradition when, following his mother's advice, he drank some milk after the race!

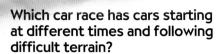

When was the first Grand Prix held?

The French Grand Prix, held at Le Mans in 1906, was the world's first race to be given the title of Grand Prix. The winner drove a Renault at an average speed of 101 kph (63 mph) to win the 1,127km (700 mile) long race.

Which car race made the world take notice of a failed automobile designer, Henry Ford?

In 1901, at a car race held at a horse racing track in Michigan, Henry Ford – in his 26 horsepower, self-designed car called Sweepstakes – defeated noted race driver Alexander Winton. The race built Ford's reputation as an automobile designer. He opened the Ford Motor Company in 1903.

What do we mean by a constructor?

The chassis (framework) builder of a Formula One car is called a constructor. The F1 world championship title for constructors was introduced in 1958. Racing teams are known by the names of their constructors.

- The Indianapolis Motor Speedway racetrack, with a tar-and-gravel surface, is also called the Brickyard because, until 1961, it was partly paved with bricks. With over 250,000 seats, it is the world's largest seating facility.

- A drag race is like an athlete's sprint run – short and fast. Cars may reach a speed of up to 400 kph (249 mph) on the approximately 402m (1,319 ft) long track!

Which car race has cars starting at different times and following difficult terrain?

Rally driving follows a difficult path that is divided into "special stages," like mud-filled roads, snow patches and slushy rivers. The cars start at different times but follow the same route, with a time limit for crossing each stage. The car with the fastest overall time wins.

The first cars were run by steam. During the late 19th and early 20th centuries, these were produced by several manufacturers. Among them were the twins Francis and Freelan Stanley, who built the "Stanley Steamer". The steam car was popular in its time, but by 1929, it was no longer being made.

Electric Energy

The electric car was developed in Europe during the 1880's. Although hugely popular, it was unable to run efficiently if the speed exceeded 32 kph (20 mph). Moreover, the battery had to be recharged after every 80 km (50 miles) of travel.

Petrol Power

Petrol-run cars appeared around 1862. By 1885, both Karl Benz and Gottlieb Daimler had built gasoline-powered cars. The year 1901 saw what is considered to be the first mass-produced car – the famous "curved-dash" Oldsmobile, developed by Ransom E. Olds.

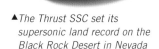

▼ This 1902 electric Studebaker could seat two passengers and had a collapsible top

Which British Royal Air Force pilot drove a car at a speed faster than sound?

RAF jet pilot Andy Green was the first person to go supersonic on land. In 1997, he drove the Thrust SSC, powered by two jet engines, achieving a top speed of 1,228 kph (763 mph).

▲ The Thrust SSC set its supersonic land record on the Black Rock Desert in Nevada

What kind of engine was used to run the first car to reach a speed exceeding 1,000 kph?

In 1983, at Nevada's Black Rock Desert, Richard Noble drove his jet engine powered car to become the first to reach a speed of some 1,018 kph (633 mph).

What makes salt flats a popular place for setting land speed records?

Salt flats, which are very popular both in Australia and America, provide a long, flat and hard surface for cars to reach a high speed quickly.

Which racer named his car "La Jamais Contente", meaning "never satisfied"?

It was Belgium's Camille Jenatzy. He had made two failed attempts to break Comte's land speed record of 62.78 kph (39 mph).Then in 1899, Jenatzy's electric car reached a new record speed of 106 kph (65.86 mph).

Which speed-record holder's father had set nine land speed records himself?

Donald Campbell's father, Malcolm Campbell, was the holder of nine land speed records.

The record-breaking Golden Arrow car was designed by J.S. Irving and driven by Henry Seagrove

Has any driver ever broken their own land speed record?

American drag racer Art Arfons had reached a speed of 698 kph (434 mph) on October 5, 1964. Just 22 days later, he drove at 863 kph (536 mph). In 1965, he set a new record of 927 kph (576 mph).

When was a car first run on an aeroplane engine?

On March 11, 1929, the Golden Arrow, powered by a Napier-Lion aeroplane engine, set a land speed record of 372 kph (231 mph) at Daytona Beach, Florida.

Which car won the first driving race?

A superior version of the first gasoline-powered car – built by the brothers Charles and Frank Duryea – was the winner in the first car race, held in Chicago, in 1895. The car was driven by Frank Duryea.

Which car set the world's first land speed record in 1898?

In 1898, a Jeantaud electric car, driven by Comte Gaston de Chasseloup-Laubat of France, set the world's first land speed record (62.78 kph, 39 mph).

Who established the first automobile factory in Italy?

In 1899, Italian industrialist Giovanni Agnelli founded Fabbrica Italini Automobili Torino (Fiat) – the first automobile factory in Italy.

What kind of record did Louis Chevrolet set?

In 1905, Louis Chevrolet set a speed record of 109 kph (68 mph) during his first race. He later designed and built the first Chevrolet car in 1911.

Which was the first experimental "car" designed by Henry Ford?

Henry Ford created his first experimental "car" in 1896. He called it a "Quadricycle" because it ran on four bicycle tyres.

▶ *The Duryea car was manufactured by Duryea Motor Wagon Company*

◀ *Camille Jenatzy set his land speed record in his streamlined car, Jamais Contente*

FACT BOX

- The "Easter Egg", a steam car built by Leon Serpollet, set a land speed record in 1902 by reaching 120.8 kph (75 mph).

▲ *The "Easter Egg" was the first non-electrically powered car to set a land speed record*

- The world's first two land speed records were set at The Flying Mile at Britain's Brooklands racing track.

- The Castrol Motor Oil Company, set up by Sir Charles Wakefield in 1899, started awarding a trophy to drivers who broke land speed records. Englishman L.G. Hornsted became the first winner when he drove his Benz at 200 kph (124 mph) in 1914.

AN OFF-ROAD DRIVE

The all-terrain vehicle (ATV) was built as a utility and recreational vehicle. It is used for purposes as varied as farming, forestry, law enforcement, adventure tourism, trail riding and camping. For people who enjoy the outdoors, the ATV allows them to venture into rugged, off-road places.

Modern ATV's are usually four-wheelers. Most of the early three-wheeled ATV's were withdrawn in the mid-1980's because they were not considered safe. Modern ATV's are designed and built to very strict safety standards, especially with regards to brake performance and vehicle stability.

Big and Bigger

ATV's come in different shapes and sizes. Some, like the Triton Predator, have as many as eight wheels for extra power and strength. Some others are relatively small, and particularly safe for young drivers. They have a reduced speed capacity and such features as a restraining strap that allows a supervising adult to stop the machine.

What are half-tracks?

First used during World War II, half-tracks are part-trucks and part-tanks meant for military use. They have tracks (like those of a tank) at the rear for travelling over broken roads and debris. The wheels at the front help them move easily.

▲ The half-track is lighter and easier to manoeuvre than a full-sized military tank

How are General Purpose (GP) vehicles better known?

The GP, developed by the U.S. Army at the start of World War II, is more commonly known as the jeep. With its strong engine and tough body, the jeep was originally designed to travel on roads damaged by warfare.

Why are ordinary cars not suitable for driving on a beach?

Often, three-wheeled vehicles (tricycles), fitted with lightweight balloon tyres, are used for driving on a beach. The wheels of an ordinary car can sink into the wet sand.

What special features can be seen in an ATV meant for safari?

A safari ATV has an extra-tough roof rack (on which a tent can be pitched) and an observation roof hatch (that can be raised for viewing wildlife).

How are victims of wars or natural disasters treated in remote places?

Aid agencies reach out to patients in mobile hospitals – specially adapted trucks fitted with medical equipment.

▲ An ATV has special features such as an extra high clearance and very large powerful wheels

◄ The tough and reliable Land Rover is popular both as a working vehicle and as a fun car

What was the top speed of the first Lunar Rover?

The top speed of the first Lunar Rover was about 11 kph (7 mph).

Which vehicle's design was based on that of the jeep?

The British Land Rover, made by the Rover Company in the 1940's, was modelled on the jeep. It was built for farmers so that they could easily travel across undeveloped country roads.

How do golfers travel around golf courses?

Golf karts, or golf buggies, are small, lightweight vehicles that carry golfers and their heavy golf clubs around the course. Driven on batteries, they cannot carry more than two people.

Why is the Lunar Rover called the "ultimate off-roader"?

The Lunar Rover's moon mission involved moving over an extremely rocky surface that also had a deep layer of sand. It had to work in an environment where there was neither air nor gravity, and experienced extreme temperature changes. It also had to be extra strong because there were no repair facilities up there!

Where was the first go-karting event held?

A go-kart is a small simple racing car with wheels. It was first made by Art Ingles using a lawnmower engine. The first go-karting event was held in 1956 in a shopping-centre car park in California, U.S.

◄ The jeep can tackle the toughest of driving conditions

US. AIR FORCE

▲ Go-karts provide plenty of fun and thrills

FACT BOX

- The Lunar Rover, carried to the Moon in 1971 by Apollo 17, was car-like, open-roofed and electric-powered.

▲ The Lunar Rover was fitted with such high-tech equipment as a satellite dish

- Off-road vehicles, or all-terrain vehicles, can easily drive across rough terrain, be it mud, desert, or stony ground. They often stand high off the ground and have sturdy bodies with large tyres.

- Off-road races are organised globally. The best-known is the 11,000 km (6,835 mile) Paris-Dakar-Cairo Rally, first held in 1978.

COLLECTOR'S CARS

Collector's cars are those that have made such a mark - usually in terms of innovation - that they are considered an indispensable part of automotive history.

Some cars are admired as symbols of innovation; some are cherished for their sheer good looks; and many others have a special place in the hearts of collectors. One of the most-loved cars is the Volkswagen Beetle. It still inspires fond feelings and is held as one of the ultimate style statements!

Brass Era Cars

The oldest types of collector's cars are popularly referred to as brass era cars. The era incorporates veteran cars, made pre-1905. These cars are extremely rare and are the prized possessions of their owners. They need constant maintenance and care.

Also incorporated are cars made between 1905 and 1919, which are called Edwardian cars because King Edward VII was the monarch of England during that time.

▲ *The Gullwing is considered to be one of the most original and outstanding cars produced by Mercedes-Benz*

What was special about the Rolls Royce Silver Ghost?

First built in 1906, the Rolls Royce Silver Ghost was a large expensive car that could be altered to suit the buyer's needs. It was last built in 1925.

How are "collector's cars" classified in terms of specific eras?

Collector's cars are often classified in terms of specific eras: these include brass era cars (pre-1918), vintage cars (1919-30) and classic cars (1930-70).

Why did the 1955 Cadillac Fleetwood have two carburettors?

The carburettor of a car feeds the fuel-air mixture into the cylinder, where it is burnt to release energy. The Cadillac needed two carburettors because it used more petrol.

How did the Rolls Royce get the name "Silver Ghost"?

During its time, the Rolls Royce Silver Ghost was hailed as a marvel of engineering. Its supremely elegant silver body and noiseless engine (which was compared to ghost-like quietness) inspired the name "Silver Ghost"!

Are antique cars ever driven by their owners?

There are tours and rallies in which antique cars in working order can participate. Veteran cars participate in a London-to-Brighton car run every year.

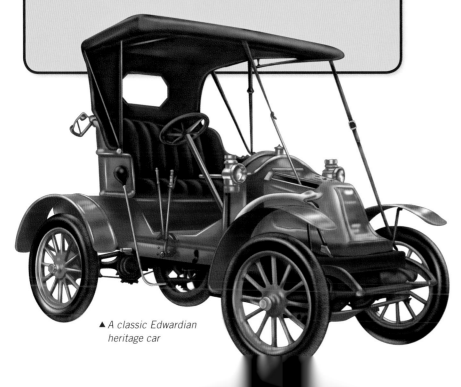

▲ *A classic Edwardian heritage car*

Which car, nicknamed "The Gullwing", was built by hand?

The 1954 Mercedes-Benz sports car was built by hand. It was the first car to have its doors opening upwards from the roof, looking somewhat like the wings of a gull! Only 1,400 were ever made.

Which 1968 car remains one of the world's fastest cars?

The 1968 Ferrari 365 GTB4 Daytona, with a top speed of 281 kph (175 mph), remains one of the world's fastest cars.

Which 1949 British car is highly valued by collectors?

The 1949 Jaguar XK 120 sports car, with a top speed of 193 kph (120 mph), is one of the most eagerly collected cars.

How long was the Cadillac Coupe de Ville?

The Cadillac Coupe de Ville, a classic American car of the 1950's, was 6m (18 feet) long. Its exceptionally long fins extended through the length of the car, and made it one of the most recognisable and innovative cars of its time.

Which American vintage car has its exhaust pipe coming out of the front bonnet?

The SJ Speedster model of the Duesenberg car has the exhaust pipe coming out of the bonnet. It is a collector's favourite and also very rare – only 36 cars were ever built!

▼ *The Duesenberg SJ Speedster is a prized collector's car that is highly valued for its quality, design and sense of luxury*

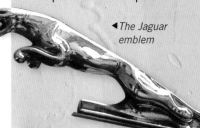

◄ *The 1968 Ferrari 365 GTB4 Daytona enjoys the status of an iconic "supercar"*

Which "classic car" created history with its smallness?

At a length of merely 3m (10 feet), the 1959 Morris Mini Minor was the most compact car of its time. It became known for its remarkable performance and an updated version is still in production today.

▲ *The Jaguar XK 120 was acclaimed for both its performance and looks*

Why did cars have fins?

In the 1950's, American cars were designed and built as showpieces of luxury and beauty. One typical feature of these cars was the fin, which was first introduced around the late 1950's. The fin got larger and larger, until it became an outstanding style feature.

FACT BOX

- Jaguar cars carry the emblem of a leaping jaguar. The third largest animal in the cat family, the jaguar is a symbol of power and speed.

◄ *The Jaguar emblem*

- Clubs such as the Antique Automobile Club of America (AACA) and FIVA (Federation Internationale Vehicules Anciens) have collectors of antique cars as their members. The clubs help members meet each other.

- When the 1957 Ford Thunderbird was first sold, buyers were given both hard and convertible tops so they could use whichever one they wanted. The car won a Lifetime Automotive Design Achievement Award in 1998.

CARS WITH A DIFFERENCE

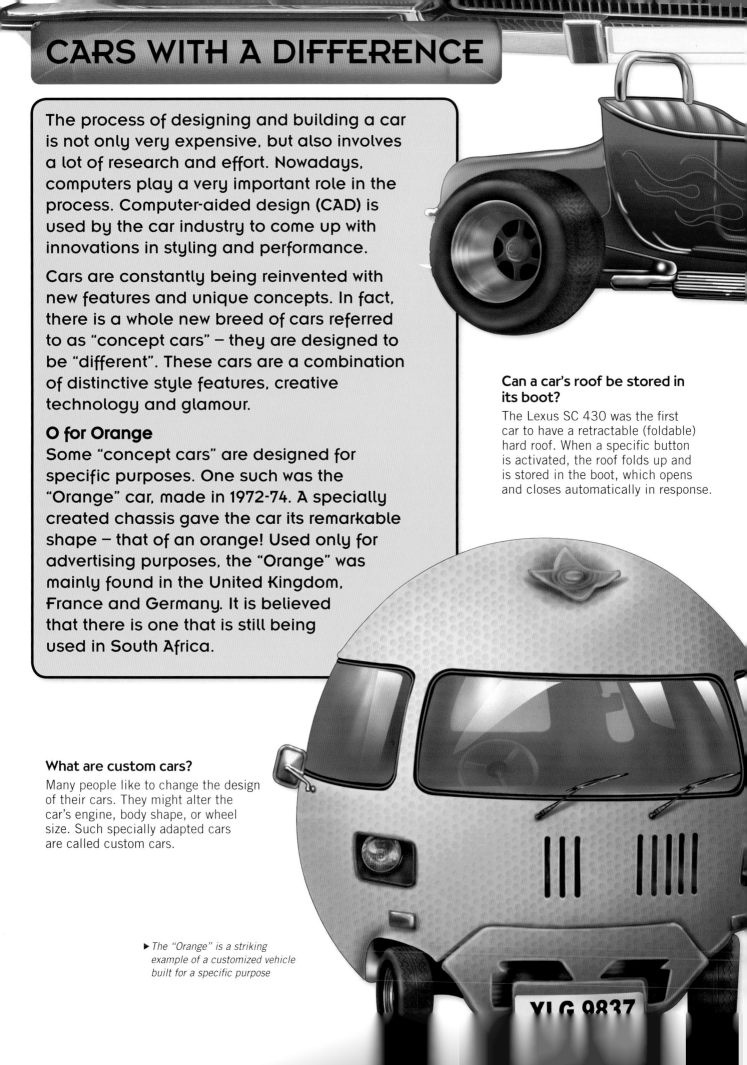

The process of designing and building a car is not only very expensive, but also involves a lot of research and effort. Nowadays, computers play a very important role in the process. Computer-aided design (CAD) is used by the car industry to come up with innovations in styling and performance.

Cars are constantly being reinvented with new features and unique concepts. In fact, there is a whole new breed of cars referred to as "concept cars" – they are designed to be "different". These cars are a combination of distinctive style features, creative technology and glamour.

O for Orange

Some "concept cars" are designed for specific purposes. One such was the "Orange" car, made in 1972-74. A specially created chassis gave the car its remarkable shape – that of an orange! Used only for advertising purposes, the "Orange" was mainly found in the United Kingdom, France and Germany. It is believed that there is one that is still being used in South Africa.

Can a car's roof be stored in its boot?

The Lexus SC 430 was the first car to have a retractable (foldable) hard roof. When a specific button is activated, the roof folds up and is stored in the boot, which opens and closes automatically in response.

What are custom cars?

Many people like to change the design of their cars. They might alter the car's engine, body shape, or wheel size. Such specially adapted cars are called custom cars.

▶ *The "Orange" is a striking example of a customized vehicle built for a specific purpose*

▼ Hot Rods are modified to improve performance and are also seen to reflect an owner's personality

Are there cars that do not look like cars at all?

Custom cars have been modified into all kinds of shapes, including a shoe, a can of beans, and even a garden shed! Such cars must be driven only after being checked for road safety and properly fitted with a horn, headlights, indicators and safety belts.

Can cars drive through water?

Amphibious cars, first built during World War II, can move through water and on land. Made by the German Amphicar Company, they can travel up to 11 kph (7 mph) in water.

▼ The Amphicar is a very useful vehicle because it functions on both land and water

FACT BOX

- Some cars are fitted with Global Positioning System (GPS) aids that are connected to satellites orbiting around Earth. The satellites send radio signals to the car about its exact position.

▲ The GPS tracking system provides cars with information about location and routes

- American car company General Motors is developing a car that can transform from a saloon car to a pick-up truck following a voice command by the driver!

- Kit cars can be made even by people who are not experts. There are kits containing all the car body and engine parts. These pieces can be put together by following an instruction booklet

Are custom cars used in car racing?

Custom cars are preferred for races in which crashes are more likely to occur. These so-called stock cars may be fitted with turbochargers for quick bursts of thrust. Custom cars are also run in drag races.

What is special about the Dream Truck?

The Dream Truck, originally owned by Spencer Murray, is a custom car that was built in the 1950's. It has fins on its body.

What special features did the Rolls Royce Phantom 3 have?

The Phantom 3 had the same engine technology as that of the aircraft engines produced by Rolls Royce. This super luxury car had special speed-sensing shock absorbers to ensure a smooth and comfortable ride.

▲ The Lexus SC 430 is a sports coupe that can be turned into a convertible within 30 seconds

Which American car had a "teardrop" motif?

The fenders, tail end and headlights of the Lincoln Zephyr – the luxury car introduced in 1936 – were teardrop-shaped.

Has a one-seater car ever been built?

The British inventor, Sir Clive Sinclair, developed a single-seater car, the electric Sinclair C5, in 1985. He believed that small, one-person cars would be a good solution to traffic problems.

▼ *The tiny Peel P50 is a three-wheeled "microcar"*

▲ *The Sinclair C5 was an environmentally friendly car that ran on batteries*

What is a "microcar"?

The earliest successful "microcar" was the Isetta. Fitted with a BMW engine, its tiny size made it both cost-effective and fuel-efficient. It was later developed into a three-wheeled car.

Was there a car without a reverse gear?

A 1964 single-seater car named the Peel P50 had a grab handle, instead of a reverse gear, attached to the back of the car. Made of ultra-light fibreglass material, the car had a speed of up to 64 kph (40 mph).

What was the "Duck" car?

The "Duck" was an amphibious car made during World War II by General Motors. The nickname comes from its original initials, DUKW. The car had six wheels and a set of propellers.

▶ *The DUKW vehicle weighed about 2,500 kg (5,511 pounds)*

A SAFE DRIVE

The car industry is constantly involved in research and development to make better, safer and more efficient cars. Modern cars have to meet many standard safety requirements, such as the strength and rigidity of side doors for ensuring passenger safety. Collapsible steering wheels reduce the danger of injury through crushing or piercing if there is a head-on collision.

A Dummy's Life

A crash-test dummy is an artificial figure made from materials that are very similar to the structure and composition of the human body. A crash dummy's spine, for instance, is made from layers of rubber pads and metallic discs so that it is almost like the actual human spine. A dummy has the very important function of simulating, or mimicking, a human being during the trauma of a car crash. Hundreds of cars, along with crash dummies, are deliberately wrecked in order to collect valuable data about the effects of collisions and accidents. All this is done to improve safety features that will protect the occupants of a car during an accident.

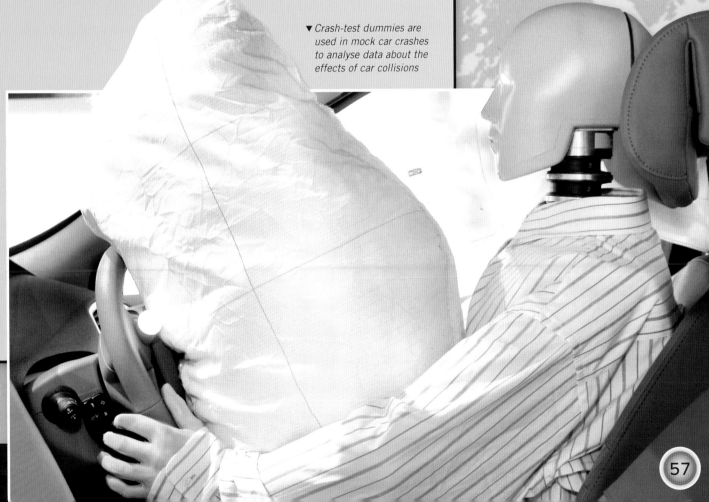

▼ Crash-test dummies are used in mock car crashes to analyse data about the effects of car collisions

What led to the introduction of traffic signals on roads?

Traffic signals were introduced to control the traffic flow. The first electric traffic light was installed in Ohio, U.S., in 1914.

What is crash glass?

Crash glass is a special type of safety glass used in cars. Even in the event of an impact, the glass does not break up into sharp and jagged pieces. It goes through a special "tempering" process that enables it to break up into small, rounded pieces without causing any injury.

Who was the first driver to be punished for driving under the influence of alcohol?

In 1897, George Smith, a taxi driver in Britain, was asked to pay a fine of one pound for drunken driving.

What purpose do air bags serve in modern cars?

Air bags first appeared in the 1980's. They inflate when the car collides with something, acting as life-saving cushions by protecting passengers when an impact throws them forward.

What is the most common method of traffic calming?

Traffic calming means slowing down traffic speed. Building speed bumps is the most common method to achieve this.

Which traffic law aimed at preventing road accidents was prevalent until 1904?

A law passed in the late 1800's required every car to have someone walk in front of it with a red flag. The driver was thereby forced to drive slowly, while the red flag warned people to move out of the car's way!

How does an air bag inflate?

An air bag has a sensor that triggers inflation when there is a collision. The inflation occurs because the air bag system produces a large amount of nitrogen gas through a chemical reaction.

What is the "crumple zone"?

Many modern cars have a "crumple zone" in the front section. This area is designed to absorb crash energy generated during a frontal collision. The body of the car "crumples" in a controlled way, so that the effect of the crash energy is lessened and the passengers are protected.

▶ *The Red Flag Act of 1865 made it compulsory for a car to have two drivers, with one person on foot carrying a red flag in front of the car*

◀ *Traffic signals*

What are the safety guidelines for a child seat?

The normal safety recommendation is that a child up to four years of age should use a child seat. For a 4-8 year old, a booster seat should be used.

Why do seat belts need to be replaced after a crash?

In most major accidents, seat belts get stretched to the maximum. The components in a seat belt that maintain the belt's tautness are usually meant for one-time use only.

◀ A child seat protects children from injuries during accidents or abrupt braking

How are cars tested for strength?

Car engineers make sample cars and conduct standard tests by hitting them against powerful robot vehicles. This helps to identify the weak points in the car's bodywork in order to make modifications accordingly.

Which invention was inspired by a cat's eyes?

In 1934, Percy Shaw, a British road repairman, invented Cat's eyes, or glass reflectors, to aid drivers by night. The idea struck him when he braked suddenly in thick fog to avoid a cat whose eyes were glowing in the dark.

FACT BOX

- Car mascots have been declared illegal because they are dangerous to pedestrians in an accident. The Rolls Royce mascot, a winged figure, folds down backwards into the bonnet when the car is in motion.

- Speedometers were introduced in cars in 1901.

- Most roads in the early 1800's were made of stone and wood blocks, which gave a rough ride. John MacAdam innovated a smoother surface in 1819 by coating roads with a hard layer of tiny stones.

◀ The famous Rolls Royce winged mascot is known as "Spirit of Ecstacy"

▶ Accident involving the "crumple zone"

There are millions of cars all over the world and each car has the capacity to be a source of air pollution. In recent years, there has been a lot of effort to reduce air pollution and clean up the environment. Governments all over the world have made laws and regulations aimed at ensuring that the problems of environmental pollution are solved. With so much concern and awareness about the dangers of pollution, car manufacturers and users have also become sensitive to the issue.

Battery Power

The electric car is an environment friendly solution to air pollution. This is increasingly being seen as the car of the future, because it will help conserve limited resources such as petrol, and also reduce increasing levels of toxins and poisonous gases in the air. It has an electric engine driven by a battery-powered controller. The technology is becoming ever more popular in the form of hybrid power, where the car has both an electric and conventional engine.

Which gas emitted by cars is considered dangerous?

Cars, while burning fuel, emit waste gases like carbon monoxide. Scientists believe that this gas traps other harmful gases in the atmosphere, making it warm. Global warming might cause glaciers to melt and low-lying areas to be submerged under water.

▲ Cars pollute the air when they let out exhaust fumes full of toxic gases

▲ An electric car provides a practical solution for conserving energy resources because it does not use petrol as fuel

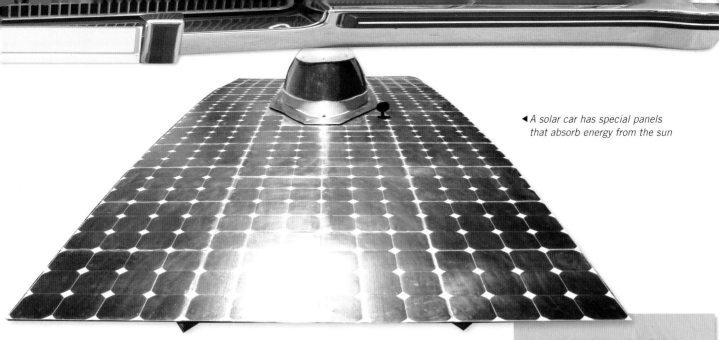

◄ A solar car has special panels that absorb energy from the sun

Do electric cars help reduce air pollution?

Electric cars do not depend on energy released from burning fuel and, hence, do not emit any harmful gases. They are powered by batteries that store electricity, and can be recharged easily with electric plugs. An electric car suffers from not having the same range of travel as conventional cars do - although the technology is ever developing.

What is the biggest risk involved in transporting oil from oil reserves to petroleum refineries?

Oil is transported in large ships from oil reserves to refineries for the extraction of petrol. If the ship sinks or leaks, oil seeps into the sea, forming a layer on the water's surface. This layer, called slick, may cause many sea creatures and birds to die.

How can old, discarded car tyres be utilized?

Car tyres are discarded once their surface pattern wears off, making them too smooth to grip the road. By shredding tyres into small rubber chips and melting them, asphalt for covering roads can be derived.

Can solar energy be tapped to run cars?

Cars run on solar energy were first developed in the 1980's. A solar-powered car, Solar Trek 1, was driven by Hans Thostrup and Larry Perkins across some 4,084 km (2,538 miles), from Perth
to Sydney in Australia.

Is it possible for a car to run on air?

An experimental car that can run on compressed air, instead of petrol or electricity, is being developed. The compressed air is contained in tanks under the car and can be refilled when necessary.

◄ The Ford Escape is a hybrid (combination) car that runs on both rechargeable batteries as well as petrol

FACT BOX

- Gasohol, a car fuel created in the late 1900's, is a mixture of lead-free petrol and ethanol prepared from grain and potatoes. Burning gasohol does not create poisonous lead fumes.

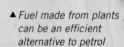

▲ Fuel made from plants can be an efficient alternative to petrol

- Compared to the older cars, the newer models are much lighter, and their efficient engines also allow them to drive much further with the same amount of fuel.

- Most car makers use recycled parts in new cars. Thus, old plastic fittings are remoulded into new designs and old batteries are used to make new ones.

▲ Petrol pumps now provide unleaded petrol for promoting a pollution-free, cleaner environment

Why do cars use "unleaded" petrol?

Unleaded petrol (that is, petrol that does not contain the metal, lead) is a safer fuel because it has a less toxic effect on the environment. Research has revealed that lead is a very dangerous air pollutant.

What is a catalytic converter?

A catalytic converter treats harmful wastes – such as hydrocarbons and carbon monoxide – produced by the exhaust from a car, converting them into harmless substances. The catalytic converter contains precious metals like palladium and platinum to aid in the process.

Why do we need an alternative to petrol for running cars?

Fumes from petrol-driven cars settle over the earth as thick layers of smog (smoke + fog). Smog causes many respiratory diseases. CNG (Compressed Natural Gas) is a good alternative to petrol, producing 20 per cent less emissions.

Why do traffic policemen wear masks?

Traffic policemen wear special anti-pollution masks to reduce the effects of breathing in exhaust fumes from vehicles. While directing traffic they are constantly exposed to high levels of pollution.

What is an oxygen sensor?

An oxygen sensor is part of a car's emissions control system and is located in the exhaust pipe. It helps a car's computer to calculate exactly how much oxygen needs to be drawn in by the engine and reduces wasteful intake.

▶ A pollution mask filters out the harmful toxins produced during heavy traffic conditions

A TALE OF SAILS

Some 5,000 years ago, the Egyptians, it is said, first built boats that helped them to cross rivers and lakes.

The Pioneers
Even earlier, however, people had learnt to make simple canoes called dugouts - tree trunks with a hollow middle and pointed ends. The Carib Indians of the Caribbean Islands called these dugouts "kanus", from where the word "canoe" is thought to be derived!

At first, people built boats by putting together bundles of reeds, tying logs into flat structures called rafts, or even with animal skin.

Sailing High
Then came faster, bigger ships with sails and oars. Soon, ships did not need oarsmen to be steered, for these could move on steam power. Today, we have ships that run on powerful engines, and even nuclear power.

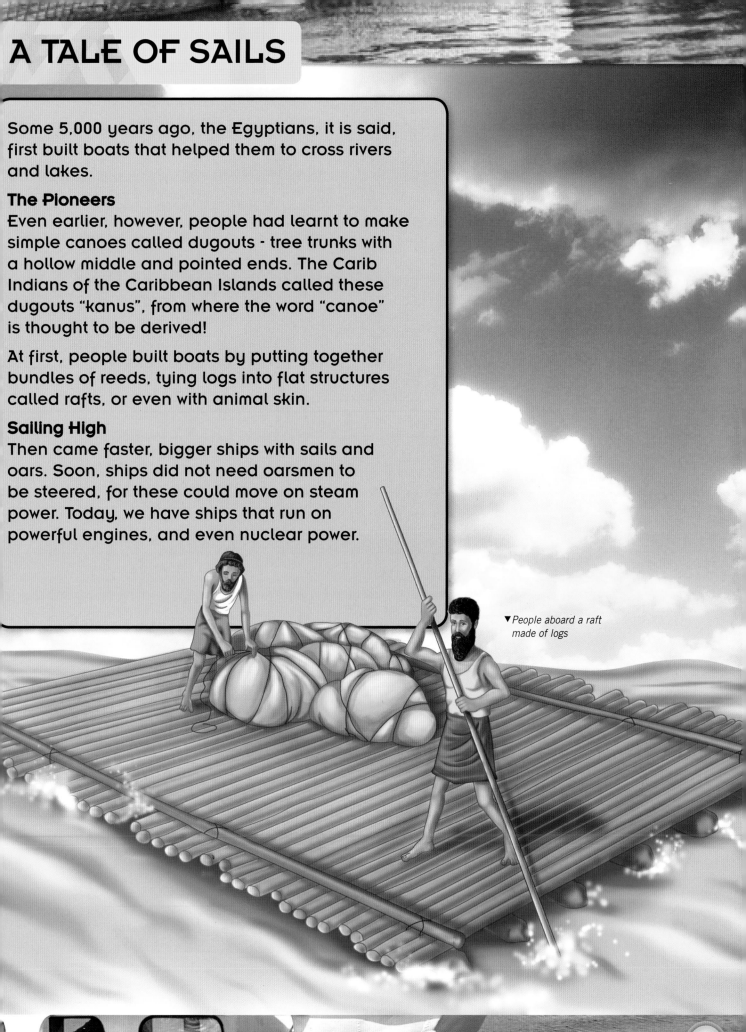

▼ People aboard a raft made of logs

Where were boats first made?

The first boats are believed to have been made in Egypt. These were fishing boats made of either papyrus reed or animal skin.

When did people begin to use sails on ships?

Over 5,000 years ago, the Egyptians began to use a square piece of cloth to catch the wind, thereby sailing. The ships also had a pair of long wooden poles (oars), which helped in steering.

Which ancient Greek ship was pointed at the prow (front)?

The trireme, a warship used by ancient Greeks, was pointed at the prow. It was used to ram holes into enemy ships during battle.

How were 19th century clippers used?

Clippers were fast-sailing ships used for trade in the mid-1800's. These had many sails for attaining greater speed.

Which was the first ship to cross the Atlantic only on steam?

In 1838, the Sirius became the first ship to cross the Atlantic on steam power alone.

▲ Steam Ship

▼ *The clipper zipped through the wind and the sea!*

Where did the trireme derive its speed from?

The fast-sailing trireme had a square sail and three lines of oarsmen (people who move the oars), one above the other. While the sail caught wind, the oarsmen rowed the ship at a surprising speed.

How did the Roman warship, quinquereme, get its name?

The quinquereme, used over 2,000 years ago, got its name from the word "quinque", which means "five". This Roman galley (warship) is believed to have had five rows of oarsmen.

What was Robert Fulton's contribution to sea navigation?

American inventor Robert Fulton founded the first steamship service in the United States. He also designed underwater weapons like submarines and torpedoes for naval warfare. One of Fulton's last contributions was the world's first steam battleship, which he named *Fulton* the First.

What were the ancient Mesopotamian rafts lined with?

The ancient Mesopotamian rafts were log platforms lined with animal skin filled with air. The hide of various animals was sewn together into a bag to make the lining.

◄ *Robert Fulton – naval pioneer*

▲ *The Clermont made its first successful trip up the Hudson River*

What kind of ships did the Romans use, about 1,800 years ago, to transport grain from Egypt?

About AD 200, the Romans used cargo ships for carrying grain from Egypt. Each ship could hold over 910,000 kg (2,006,206 pounds) of grain, besides about 1,000 passengers.

▶ *The trireme represented the sea power of the ancient Greeks*

Which was the first successful steamboat?

The *Clermont*, built by Robert Fulton in 1807, was the first-ever successful river steamboat.

How did the ancient Egyptians carry obelisks (large stones) down the Nile?

The ancient Egyptians used wooden ships called barges to ferry huge obelisks across the River Nile. The biggest barges could carry about 680 tonnes of cargo!

FACT BOX

● There were no passenger ships in ancient Rome. People usually travelled on cargo ships. These ships had a few cabins for important people, while the other passengers made place for themselves on the deck.

● In order to make dugouts, the early people hollowed out tree trunks. They did this either by using stone tools or by burning away the excess wood.

● The people of ancient Mesopotamia made boats by lashing bundles of reed together. They covered the boats with a layer of bitumen (a tar-like substance) to make them waterproof.

▲ *A Mesopotamian reed boat*

RAIDERS AND ROBBERS

Over 1,200 years ago, Norsemen from Scandinavia began leaving their homeland in search of better farmland. Many of them became fierce raiders and terrorised the rest of Europe. These warriors came to be known as Vikings.

Sea Sovereigns

The Vikings were expert shipbuilders who sailed on their swift wooden ships to different places. They set up trade centres and discovered new routes too. They traded walrus and narwhal ivory, furs, birds and live polar bears for goods like timber and grain. It is said that the Vikings who settled in Russia were called "Rus". Hence the name Russia!

Pirates of the Sea

For centuries, ships have been attacked and plundered on high seas. Such attacks were especially common from the 1500's to the 1700's. Merchant ships crossing the Caribbean and the Mediterranean Sea were often targeted. The raiders were called pirates.

Armed with pistols and knives, the pirates sailed forth on small, light ships. They fired at the merchant vessels, gave them a chase, and moved their own ships next to them. Tying the ships together with hooks and ropes, they then boarded the merchant ships. The booty often consisted of valuable gold and silver objects.

▲ A pirate's pistol and a skull-and-crossbones hat

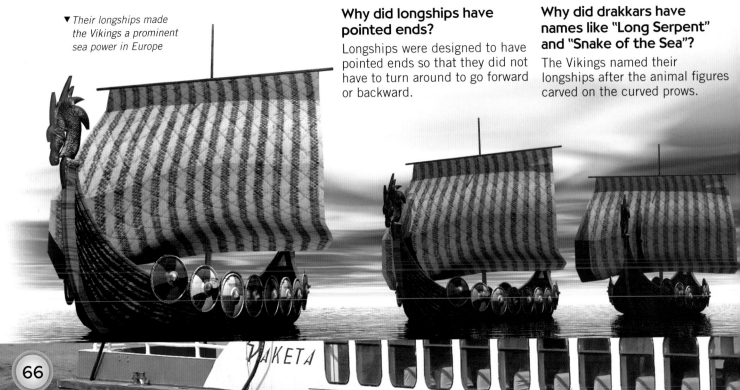

▼ Their longships made the Vikings a prominent sea power in Europe

Why did longships have pointed ends?

Longships were designed to have pointed ends so that they did not have to turn around to go forward or backward.

Why did drakkars have names like "Long Serpent" and "Snake of the Sea"?

The Vikings named their longships after the animal figures carved on the curved prows.

Which navigation tool did the Vikings use to sail during the day?

The Vikings used a sunboard during the day for navigating in the right direction. It worked like a sundial, measuring the height of the sun at different times of the day.

Who built light and swift longships about 10 centuries ago?

The Vikings built longships, which were also called "drakkars" (dragon ships). These wooden ships were the fastest of their time.

Who was Captain Kidd?

Captain Kidd was a pirate hunter who, according to legend, captured a ship full of treasure and then hid the booty on a deserted island. However, he could not come back for the treasure as he was soon caught and punished. It is believed the buried treasure chest was never found.

What did the booty collected by pirates consist of?

The loot collected by pirates usually consisted of such valuable objects as silk, jewels, spices and ivory.

How did the Vikings build their ships?

The Vikings built their ships with overlapping planks of wood. They made the ships waterproof by painting them with tar from pine trees.

▼ *The fabled treasure of Captain Kidd*

Which Viking ships could come right up onto the beach from the sea?

The longships could come right up onto the beach from the sea, thus enabling the Vikings to jump off and start fighting straightaway.

How did the longships move when there was little or no wind?

Each longship had about 15 to 40 pairs of oars, which were used to row the ship when there was little or no wind.

Which famous pirate wore his beard in braids?

A fierce pirate, Edward Teach, plaited his long, black beard. He even got a nickname for this – "Blackbeard!"

What were pirate ships of the 16th and 17th centuries armed with?

The pirate ships of the 1500's and the 1600's were armed with large cannons that fired lead balls at merchant vessels.

▲ *More than 20 cannons could be mounted on a large pirate ship!*

▲ *Spears, swords and battle-axes comprised the main weapons of the Vikings*

Did the Vikings carry weapons on their ships?

The Vikings carried swords, spears, axes, bows and arrows as they sailed to different lands in their longships. They were also armed with round wooden shields.

▼ *A pirate flag was meant to invoke fear*

FACT BOX

- Not all ships made by the Vikings were huge. The "knorrs", or ships used for trade, were only about 15m (49 ft) long – almost half the length of a longship.

- Each pirate in a group had a rank. While the leader got the maximum share of the loot, the others divided it according to their ranks.

- The Jolly Roger flag was used by many groups of pirates in the 1700's. The flag showed a white skull and a pair of crossbones against a black background. Skulls and skeletons were commonly featured in other pirate flags too.

ON THE SAIL TRAIL

The sea opened a whole new world, as people set sail for distant, unknown lands. They were the explorers.

Many Tides Ago
The Egyptians are known to have sailed across the Red Sea to bring home precious metals, myrrh and wood. We know little about their travels though.

Marco Polo, the Italian, visited China in the 1200's. He later described, in a book, the Chinese wonders like silk, paper and gunpowder, which were still unknown in Europe.

The Age of Discovery
In the 15th century, traders used to bring silk, spices and precious gemstones from the Indies (in Asia) through a land route, which later become dangerous. It was important to find a direct sea route.

In 1492, Christopher Columbus set sail from Spain towards the west, hoping to reach the Indies, When he landed on the Caribbean Islands, he thought he had reached India. So he called the native people "Indians"! The islands came to be called the West Indies.

▲ The exquisite gemstones of Asia lured European traders in hordes

Who made the first around-the-world trip?

The sailors aboard the ship Victoria were the first to travel around the world. The owner of the ship, Ferdinand Magellan, died before the completion of the trip, which took approximately three years.

What does the earliest known record of exploration describe?

The earliest known record of exploration describes the adventures of Hannu, an ancient Egyptian explorer who went across the Red Sea in about 2750 B.C. The record is carved in rock.

◀ Portuguese navigator Magellan set sail from Spain on September 20, 1519

VAKETA

Which ship did Captain Cook sail on his voyage to Australia, New Zealand and the Pacific Islands?

Captain Cook sailed the 30m (100 ft) long *Endeavour* on his southern voyage. The lowest of the ship's three decks was used for storing supplies for the long journey.

Who designed the caravel ship?

The Portuguese, who were keen sailors, designed the caravel. This small ship was a combination of the European and Arabic ship-building styles.

▲ *The caravel was widely used for exploration during the 15th and 16th centuries*

◄ *Marco Polo wrote a famous book, Il milione ("The Million"), about his travels*

FACT BOX

- During the time when Captain Cook sailed to Australia and the Pacific Islands, there were no cameras. So he took a group of artists with him, in order to bring back sketches of plants and animals of foreign shores.

- The *Kon Tiki*, a wooden raft, sailed a distance of 6,920 km (4,300 miles) – from Peru to Raroia (in Polynesia) – in 101 days.

- Vasco da Gama was the first European to reach India by sea. He had made the voyage to bring back Indian spices. Europeans used these spices to flavour rotten meat, so that people would not realise it was spoilt!

How long did Marco Polo's trip to China last?

Marco Polo set sail for the long voyage to China in 1271, and returned home to Italy in 1295, after 24 years!

Which famous explorer sailed further south than anybody before him?

In 1768, Captain James Cook set sail for the South Pacific, further south than anybody before him. Over a period of three years, Captain Cook charted 8,000 km (4,970 miles) of coastline.

What were the special eatables that Captain Cook served his sailors on the voyage?

Pickled cabbage and orange extracts were served to the sailors aboard the Endeavour. Rich in Vitamin C, these food items protected them from a disease called scurvy.

▲ *The Portuguese were the first to bring spices from India to Europe*

What kind of sails were used on the ships of Vasco da Gama?

Vasco da Gama's ships were small and had square as well as lateen (triangular) sails. This made the ships easy to sail, even on rough seas.

Which three ships made up Christopher Columbus' fleet on his historic voyage of 1492?

The *Nina*, the *Pinta*, and the *Santa Maria* made up Christopher Columbus' fleet on his voyage of discovery to the West Indies, in 1492.

Which famous tea-carrying clipper was owned by a man popularly known as "White Hat Willis"?

The famous *Cutty Sark* was owned by John Willis, who got the popular nickname because he always wore a white-coloured top hat.

Why did Columbus leave the Santa Maria midway through his voyage?

The *Santa Maria* was wrecked on the way, which is why Columbus had to complete the rest of the journey aboard the Nina.

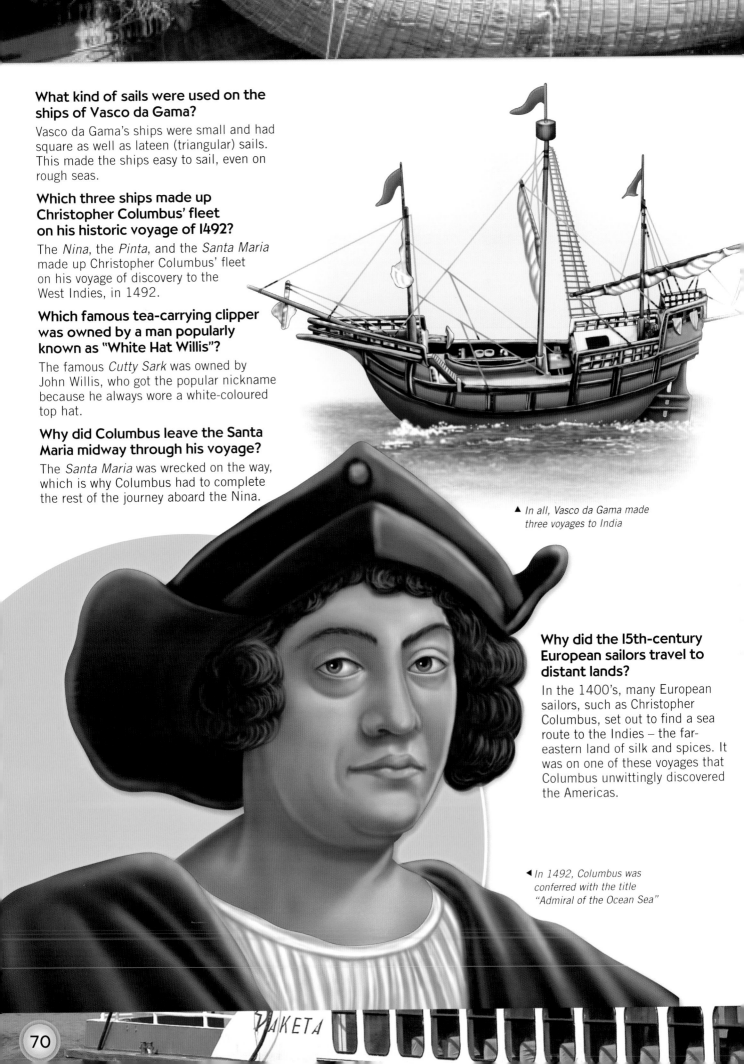

▲ In all, Vasco da Gama made three voyages to India

Why did the 15th-century European sailors travel to distant lands?

In the 1400's, many European sailors, such as Christopher Columbus, set out to find a sea route to the Indies – the far-eastern land of silk and spices. It was on one of these voyages that Columbus unwittingly discovered the Americas.

◀ In 1492, Columbus was conferred with the title "Admiral of the Ocean Sea"

SAIL MY BOAT

Before there were sails, oars or paddles, people used to steer their animal-skin boats using only their hands!

Poles Apart

Before long, people realised that they could push the riverbed with a long pole, and move the boat far more easily. This method worked only in shallow waters though.

Soon, somebody thought of making one end of the pole flat and wide. Thus the paddle was invented. Next, paddles were attached to the sides of the boats. These became known as oars.

Steam Power

The invention of the sail made it possible for people to go on long sea voyages. The sail was a large piece of cloth that could catch the wind and propel the boat.

However, sails depended entirely on the force of the wind. Steam engines powered by coal presented a more effective way to run ships. Now we have ships with propellers to cut through the water, and ones with wing-like foils too.

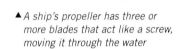

▲ A ship's propeller has three or more blades that act like a screw, moving it through the water

What is an anchor used for?

An anchor is a heavy object that is used to hold a ship in place. The object is attached to a chain, one end of which is tied to the ship, while the other lowers the anchor down to the bottom of the river or the sea.

Which part of a boat catches wind, so that it sails through water?

Wind blows across the sail of a boat, pushing the craft ahead. A long pole, called the mast, holds the sail in place.

What is the main body of a ship called?

The main body of a ship is called the hull. The bow is the front portion of the ship, while the stern is the rear.

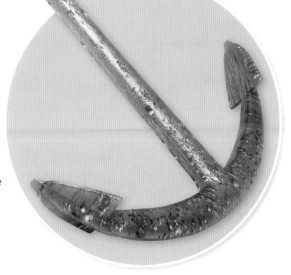

▶ Prior to the modern metal anchors, ships earlier used large stones or sackfuls of sand!

Are there any boats that move without a sail?

Rowing boats and canoes do not use any sail, because they do not rely on the wind. They have oars, or paddles, that move them forward.

▼ *The canoe is a lightweight boat that is widely used for recreation or sport*

Why are lighthouses important to sailors?

Lighthouses help sailors locate their position as well as steer clear of rocks. These emit bright beams of light at regular intervals for signalling to ships.

What happens if the wind drops while a sailing boat is far from the shore?

Modern sailing boats are usually fitted with engines or outboard motors so that they can power themselves in the case of there being no wind.

◄ *Back in the 4th century A.D., the Romans are said to have had about 30 lighthouse towers!*

What are the things that a sailor must carry as safety gear?

A sailor must have a bucket aboard to bail out water, in case the hull develops a hole. There should also be a paddle to row the boat to safety, should the wind drop. All crew members must also wear life jackets.

Why is it essential for ships to carry lifeboats?

Ships carry lifeboats so that passengers can be rowed to safety in case the ship meets with an accident and starts sinking.

What did the sailors of olden times consult for navigation?

The sailors in earlier times relied heavily on the position of the stars in the sky to find their way. They also used magnetic compasses to find out the direction in which they were sailing.

▲ *Radar can detect, locate and identify various kinds of objects at a long distance*

▼ *In the 12th century, Chinese and European mariners had learnt to use a form of magnetic compass*

Why did sailors in the l5th century keep backstaffs on their ships?

In the 15th century, sailors used an instrument called the backstaff to determine the position of the ship. The backstaff told them how far the ship was from the equator.

How do modern-day sailors find their way on a long voyage?

Modern-day sailors use navigation satellites that guide the computers on the ship. Radar systems help them avoid running into other ships.

Which instrument helps sailors keep time accurately?

The chronometer tells sailors the exact time, thereby enabling them to calculate the position of the ship accurately.

▼ *The helm of a sailing boat*

Today, ships are no longer just a means of travel and transport. They are used for a variety of other purposes as well.

Cargo Carriers

Every day, thousands of ships travel on seas, oceans and other waterways carrying cargo – from petroleum, oil, wine, meat, vegetables and fresh fruits to aeroplanes and trains! Since eatables can easily get spoilt, these are ferried on refrigerated ships.

Uses Galore!

Did you know that ships help in cleaning lakes and rivers? These ships have a huge arm attached to their hulls. As the arm is lowered down to the bottom of a river or a lake, it scoops out the dirt. Ships are used to break through huge ice blocks in the sea around the poles, as well as in laying telephone and telegraph wires along the ocean floor. Without these wires, it would have been impossible to make phone calls from one country to another!

▼ Metal containers for holding a ship's cargo

Which ships are used to cut through thick ice in cold regions?

Icebreakers cut through ice in the snowcapped polar regions and thus pave the way for other ships to pass through.

What are the different types of ships?

Ships are divided into various types – such as passenger, cargo, service, sport and fishing ships – based on the uses they are put to.

▶ Icebreakers have a markedly sloping bow, strong steel plating and extremely powerful engines

Which boat has a pair of "wings"?

The hydrofoil has a pair of wing-like foils attached to it. The foils lift the hull just off the surface, making the boat glide through the water.

▼ Hydrofoils can travel at a speed of over 113 km (70 miles) per hour

What is the largest ship in the world?

Knock Nevis is the largest ship in the world and is now used as an immobile offshore platform for the oil industry. At 458m (1,504 ft) in length it is longer than the Empire State Building laid on its side!

What is a dredge used for?

A dredge is a service vessel used to dig up sediments from lagoons as well as the sea floor. Dredges are also used for collecting and carrying sand to beaches.

What are ro-ro ships?

Ro-ro ships are roll-on/roll-off cargo ships, which carry containers as well as cars, trucks and even trains. Long platforms (ramps) on wheels are used to roll cargo on and off these ships.

Which ship carries people over long distances, on voyages that last many days?

Passenger liners carry people over long distances, even from one continent to another! Luxury liners have all kinds of facilities, such as film theatres, swimming pools and dining bars on-board.

▼ The Queen Mary 2 (QM2), as it set sail on January 12, 2004, become the largest, longest and most expensive passenger liner ever built!

▼ Coal

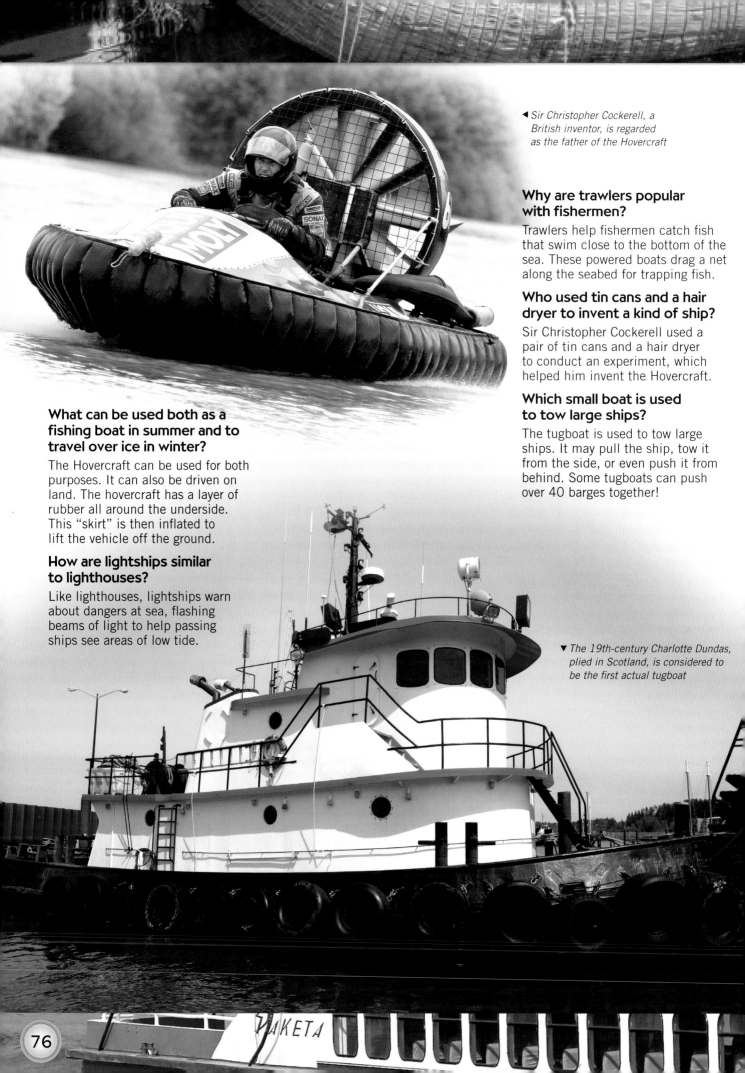

Sir Christopher Cockerell, a British inventor, is regarded as the father of the Hovercraft

Why are trawlers popular with fishermen?

Trawlers help fishermen catch fish that swim close to the bottom of the sea. These powered boats drag a net along the seabed for trapping fish.

Who used tin cans and a hair dryer to invent a kind of ship?

Sir Christopher Cockerell used a pair of tin cans and a hair dryer to conduct an experiment, which helped him invent the Hovercraft.

Which small boat is used to tow large ships?

The tugboat is used to tow large ships. It may pull the ship, tow it from the side, or even push it from behind. Some tugboats can push over 40 barges together!

What can be used both as a fishing boat in summer and to travel over ice in winter?

The Hovercraft can be used for both purposes. It can also be driven on land. The hovercraft has a layer of rubber all around the underside. This "skirt" is then inflated to lift the vehicle off the ground.

How are lightships similar to lighthouses?

Like lighthouses, lightships warn about dangers at sea, flashing beams of light to help passing ships see areas of low tide.

The 19th-century Charlotte Dundas, plied in Scotland, is considered to be the first actual tugboat

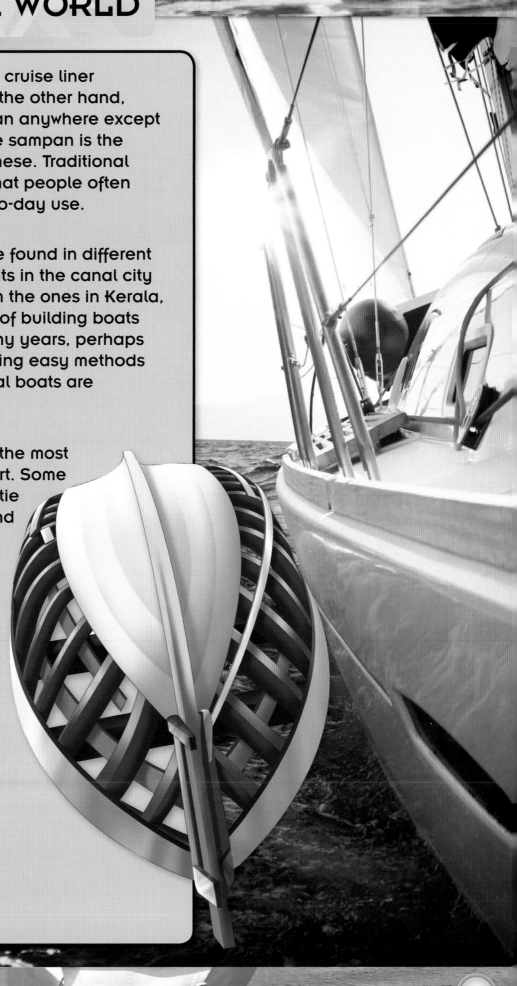

AROUND THE WORLD

You may spot a passenger cruise liner anywhere in the world. On the other hand, you will never see a sampan anywhere except in Asia! This is because the sampan is the traditional boat of the Chinese. Traditional boats are simple vessels that people often make themselves for day-to-day use.

Building Boats

Different kinds of boats are found in different parts of the world. The boats in the canal city of Venice are different from the ones in Kerala, India. Traditional methods of building boats have endured through many years, perhaps even centuries. Despite using easy methods and simple tools, traditional boats are very sturdy.

All-Purpose Boats

In some places, boats are the most important mode of transport. Some people are even known to tie their boats in one place and live in them! Others use their boats as shops for selling their wares.

▶ The wooden frame of a boat

Which materials are used in the traditional canoes of Marshall Islands in the Pacific?

The traditional Marshallese canoes are made of logs from the breadfruit tree. The logs are tied together with coconut string. The sails come from the dried, sword-shaped leaves of the pandanus tree.

Where are dhows from?

The dhow is an Arabian boat made of wooden planks sewn together. It was first used – many centuries ago – by Indian and Arab merchants.

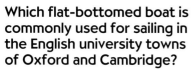

Which flat-bottomed boat is commonly used for sailing in the English university towns of Oxford and Cambridge?

The punt is a long, narrow and flat-bottomed boat that is commonly seen at the rivers in Oxford and Cambridge. The boat is propelled with a long pole.

What is a coracle?

A coracle is a small boat, which looks like a wicker basket, with room for one. Mainly a fishing boat, the coracle has been used in many countries for thousands of years.

In which country can you find a boat called a junk?

Junks are strong ships used as houses, or even schools, in many parts of China. These ships – with large sails made of linen or matting – are used to carry cargo too.

Where in the world are gondolas found?

Gondolas are long, flat-bottomed boats with high sterns and prows commonly used in the canals of Venice.

▼ Reeds, grasses or saplings are used to make the bowlshaped coracle

▼ A gondola is steered with a single oar at the stern

Which boats are not usually used for sailing?

Houseboats, or floating houses, are tied to a fixed place and not usually used for sailing. Built on rivers and canals, these boats serve as houses or hotels. Wooden houseboats are a common sight in the Kashmir Valley of India.

What kinds of boats are sailed on Lake Titicaca in South America?

Reed boats, made from bundles of totora reed, are sailed on Lake Titicaca. These small, porous boats have a square sail and are steered with a long oar.

▲ Houseboats are a popular tourist attraction in Kashmir, India

◀ It is mostly the Thai women who can be seen paddling their boats at the "talaat naam"

Which long boat, built by the Inuit people, usually carries only one person?

The kayak built by the Inuits usually has room for only one person. This boat has a strong wooden frame, covered with seal or caribou skin.

What is the term for the long and narrow canoe sailed on Indonesian waters?

The long, narrow canoe sailed in Indonesia is called the prau. It is curved and pointed at both ends.

What weapons did the Inuit people carry on their kayaks?

The Inuits carried harpoons on their kayaks to hunt animals. In fact, the deck of the kayak had a harpoon rest fitted on it.

What happens at the "talaat naam" in Thailand?

Thailand has floating markets called "talaat naam". Shopkeepers row their wooden boats – laden with fruits, vegetables, flowers and other wares – along the waterways.

◀ The Inuit people used the kayak both for fishing and hunting

FACT BOX

- The *Al Hashemi II*, which is the world's largest wooden dhow, is held together by about 80,000 kg (176,369 lbs) of nails and bolts. The ship serves as a venue for meetings.

- The Chinese sampan gets its name from the words "sam" and "pan", which mean "three planks" in English.

- The people of the ancient Greek civilisation painted eyes on their boats for good luck. They believed that their protecting gods could see ahead through these painted eyes.

▼ The eye motif can be seen on some Greek boats even today

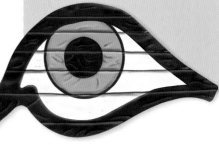

WAR AT SEA

As far back as Ancient Egyptian times, warfare has been conducted at sea. The forces that fought at sea came to be known as naval forces, or the navy.

Many Wars

Around 2,500 years ago, the city-state of Athens had the largest navy in ancient Greece. The triremes – fast ships with pointed prows – could smash holes into enemy ships.

Then, in the 1500's, warships began to be armed. These vessels, built by the Spanish, were called "galleons" and carried cannons and guns.

In 1588, the British defeated the powerful Spanish Armada by a clever trick. They loaded a few ships with gunpowder, set them on fire, and then sent them sailing towards the Spanish fleet.

Weapons in War

Most modern navies possess fleets of ships, some large enough to carry several aircraft! While some ships carry troops and weapons across the sea, others sail close to the shore to protect the areas around it. Warships are usually armed with weapons like missiles and torpedoes.

▶ Most ancient and medieval catapults had wooden beams

Where was the first organised navy created?

About 4,300 years ago, the Egyptians developed the first organised navy in the world.

Which was the first submarine to sink a ship during war?

In 1864, the propeller-powered *Hunley*, of the U.S. navy, became the first submarine to sink an enemy ship during war. After sinking the USS *Housatonic*, the *Hunley* sank too.

▼ Cornelis Drebbel, a 17th-century Dutch inventor, is widely believed to have built the first submarine

▲ Torpedoes are underwater missiles that explode on touching the hull of a ship or a submarine

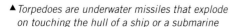

◄An ocean minesweeper is usually about 50m (165 ft) long

Why are submarines an important part of a nation's navy?

Submarines remain hidden underwater, carrying deadly missiles like torpedoes. Patrol submarines seek and destroy enemy ships. The earliest submarines were round, drum-like vessels made of wood.

What did ancient navies use catapults for?

Ancient naval forces used catapults to fire stones and hot coals at enemy vessels.

Which ships are used by navies to fight wars?

Navies use a variety of warships, such as aircraft carriers, battleships, cruisers, destroyers, frigates, minesweepers and submarines.

How do minesweepers help in defending a country?

Minesweepers are naval vessels used to find and destroy mines laid by enemy forces.

Which submarine carries a missile that could cause mass devastation?

Nuclear missile-carrying submarines are armed with powerful nuclear missiles capable of causing mass devastation. The role of these submarines is as a deterrent and it is improbable that the missiles will ever be used.

◄Diving bell – a mechanism by which a diver can move between the water surface and the lower depths

▲ *The deck of an aircraft carrier allows both take-offs and landings by a plane*

What are frigates and destroyers used for?

Frigates and destroyers are fast-moving warships armed with missiles and other weapons to attack enemy aircraft and submarines.

When were the largest-ever twin battleships destroyed?

The largest-ever twin battleships, Yamato and Musashi of Japan, were destroyed during World War II (1939- 45).

▶ *Modern frigates are frequently used to carry helicopters to help in locating submarines*

How do submarines find enemy ships that are sailing on the surface?

The captain of a submarine can see the water surface through a special device called a periscope. Submarines are also equipped with sonar (sound navigation and ranging), which helps in locating other submarines.

Which warship, before the invention of aircraft carriers, used to be the most heavily armed?

Before aircraft carriers were built, battleships used to carry the maximum amount of weapons. These large warships carried powerful guns to fire at enemy vessels.

SAILING SPORT

Boating is popular all over the world. People take part in boat races to see who rows faster. Some races have hundreds of people rowing a single boat!

Playing with the Wind

As you know, sailing boats have sails that catch wind and move the boat. A skilful sailor sees to it that wind moves over the sails in the right way. If the sailor does not know how to adjust the sails, the boat may move very slowly even on a windy day.

Adventure and Action

For the adventurous, there are sports, such as white-water rafting, in which they paddle rafts on swirling white waters (rapids). The rafts, made of nylon and rubber, are rectangular with rounded sides. Rowing kayaks on rapids is also a popular sport. Double-bladed paddles are used to row these boats.

Motor Fun

Motorboats race on waterways at great speed. These boats have powerful engines. Motorboat racing is also an exciting spectator sport enjoyed by many.

▼ *Double-bladed paddles*

▲ *Rafting through the rapids*

What kinds of obstacles must white-water rafters avoid while paddling?

Rafters have to steer their rafts away from rocks hidden in the fast-flowing rivers, as well as sharp drops and large swirls that might threaten to overturn the raft.

◀ *The life jacket is essential protective gear for adventures on water*

Why are life jackets worn by sailors sleeveless?

Most life jackets are made without sleeves so that sailors can move their arms freely.

What keeps life jackets afloat on water?

Life jackets are filled with light materials, such as foam, or gasses, which keep them afloat.

What is the function of the "kill switch" found on most motorboats?

The "kill switch" is attached to the life jacket of a motorboat sailor. In the event of the sailor being thrown off the boat, the switch turns off the motor, thus preventing the boat from going out of control and injuring the sailor.

How many oars does a person need to scull a boat?

A person needs two oars to scull a boat. Rowing a boat with two oars, one on either side, is called sculling.

How old is the sport of windsurfing?

Windsurfing is said to date back to ancient times. However, the modern version was invented in the 1960's by Schweitzer and Drake, two surfers from California, U.S. They thought of a basic design for a sailboard – a surfboard with a mast and a triangle-shaped sail that could be moved in any direction.

▼ *The first World Windsurfing Championship was held in 1973*

Which sailing trophy is also the world's oldest trophy in international sport?

The America's Cup, awarded to the winner of a sailing competition between two countries, is the world's oldest trophy in international sport. It was first awarded in 1851.

FACT BOX

- The America's Cup was named in honour of the U.S. yacht, America, after the yacht beat 14 British yachts in a race in 1851.

- Part of a sailor's safety gear is the floating, doughnut-shaped buoy. A person can hold on to the buoy to stay afloat until help comes along.

- The pram is a small sailing boat assembled at home using a kit. The pram is so called because it has blunt ends, just like those of baby carriages.

▲ *Ring buoys*

▲ Snake-boat races are held
during the harvest festival
in August/September

▼ Catamarans are lightweight
and fast through the water

Which is the largest team sport in the world?

The snake-boat racing held in Kerala, India, is the largest team sport in the world. The long snake-boat has room for about 150 people.

How old is the famous boat race between Oxford and Cambridge universities?

The boat race between the two universities dates back to 1829. Teams of rowers race over a 6.8 km (4.25 mile) stretch of the River Thames in London.

Which racing boat has two hulls?

The raft-like catamaran has two hulls. This lightweight boat may be powered by both sail and engine.

Who is the "helm" on a sailing boat?

The "helm" is a person who controls the direction of the sailing boat as well as instructs the rest of the crew.

What are handicap races?

Handicap races are those sailing races in which small boats compete with larger ones.

DIVE TO DISCOVER

How do we know about ships that sank hundreds of years ago? Trained people called marine archaeologists dive deep down and study the wrecks of ships that lie on the seabed. Shipwrecks may still hold many valuables, such as coins, jewels, luggage and furniture, besides the remains of the ship.

Diving Down the Ages

Thousands of years ago, people are believed to have dived underwater by using reeds and bamboo shoots as snorkels. The ancient Greeks and Romans explored the sea depths by holding their breath, fetching sponges, shells and pearls. The invention of the diving bell made it possible to breathe underwater. Over the years, fins, snorkels and goggles for divers were developed. Diving suits became waterproof and lighter. Vehicles called submersibles carry people to depths where swimmers cannot reach. Today, divers can dive underwater to repair ships, collect samples and conduct research.

▼ Jewels – treasures from the depths!

Why is the Bermuda Triangle also known as the Devil's Triangle?

The mysterious disappearance of about 50 ships and 20 aeroplanes in the Bermuda Triangle led people to call it the Devil's Triangle.

After which ship is the Jonathan Rock, off the Californian coast, named?

The Jonathan Rock is named after *Brother Jonathan* – a ship that sank on hitting the rock on July 30, 1865.

Which "unsinkable" passenger liner sank on its first voyage?

The Titanic, a luxury liner hailed as the "unsinkable ship", sank on its very first voyage, on April 14-15, 1912. It was sailing from Southampton, England, to New York City, U.S.

◄ The Bermuda Triangle is an area of the North Atlantic Ocean located off North America

NORTH AMERICA
BERMUDA
BERMUDA ISLAND

WEST INDIES

Straits

JAMAICA

Caribbean Sea

Why did the *Titanic* sink?

The hull of the *Titanic* was ripped apart when it hit a massive iceberg in the North Atlantic. Within three hours the ship sank, killing over 1,500 people on-board.

What kind of an underwater vehicle is the *Trieste*?

The *Trieste* is a vehicle especially designed for deep-sea diving. This type of vehicle is known as a bathyscaphe.

▼ On September 1, 1985, the wreck of the Titanic was found at a depth of nearly 4,000m (13,000 ft)

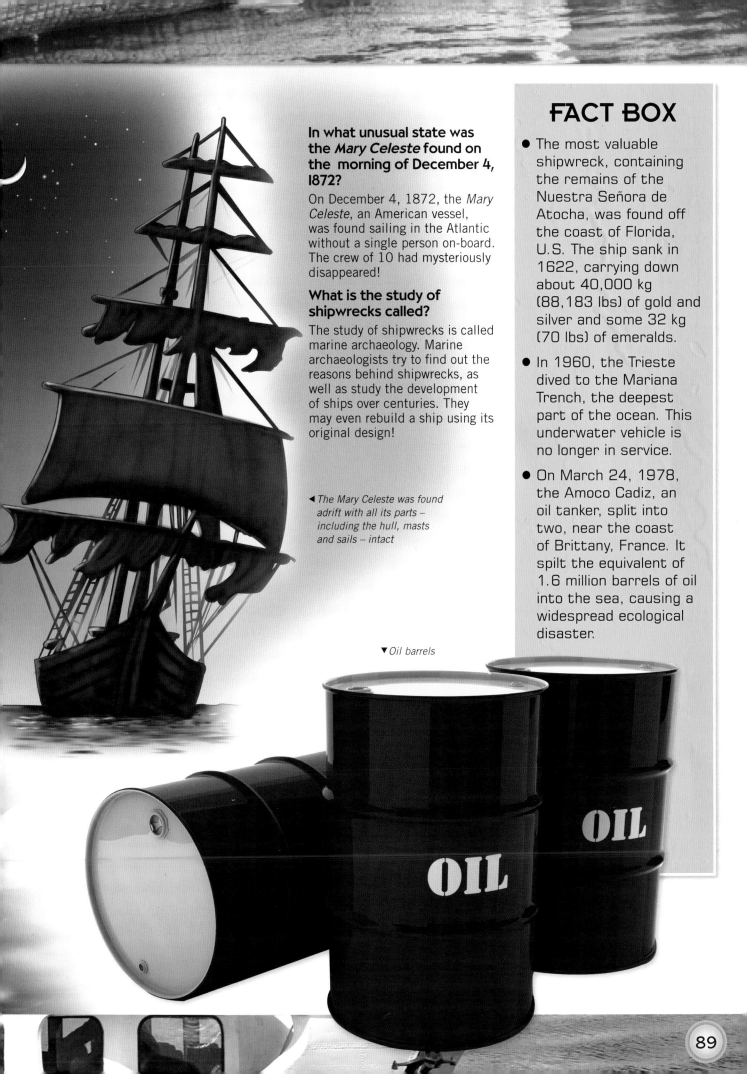

In what unusual state was the *Mary Celeste* found on the morning of December 4, 1872?

On December 4, 1872, the *Mary Celeste*, an American vessel, was found sailing in the Atlantic without a single person on-board. The crew of 10 had mysteriously disappeared!

What is the study of shipwrecks called?

The study of shipwrecks is called marine archaeology. Marine archaeologists try to find out the reasons behind shipwrecks, as well as study the development of ships over centuries. They may even rebuild a ship using its original design!

◄ *The Mary Celeste was found adrift with all its parts – including the hull, masts and sails – intact*

▼ *Oil barrels*

FACT BOX

- The most valuable shipwreck, containing the remains of the Nuestra Señora de Atocha, was found off the coast of Florida, U.S. The ship sank in 1622, carrying down about 40,000 kg (88,183 lbs) of gold and silver and some 32 kg (70 lbs) of emeralds.

- In 1960, the Trieste dived to the Mariana Trench, the deepest part of the ocean. This underwater vehicle is no longer in service.

- On March 24, 1978, the Amoco Cadiz, an oil tanker, split into two, near the coast of Brittany, France. It spilt the equivalent of 1.6 million barrels of oil into the sea, causing a widespread ecological disaster.

How do robot submersibles capture pictures of underwater life?

Some robot submersibles are fitted with a camera and powerful lights that film underwater scenes.

Which submersibles do not carry people on-board?

A robot submersible does not carry people on-board. Some submersibles may even have arms for collecting underwater samples!

What is a manned submersible?

A manned submersible is one that takes people on underwater expeditions.

What were the *Galeones de Tierra Firme* and the *New Spain Flota* carrying when they sank in 1715?

The two Spanish fleets were carrying a large dowry of jewels for Elizabeth Farnesse, who had married the Spanish king, Felipe V.

Which was the first vehicle to go beneath the ice shelves of the Antarctic region?

The £5m Autosub, an unmanned submersible, was the first to survey the region beneath the thick Antarctic ice shelves. This robot submarine runs on batteries.

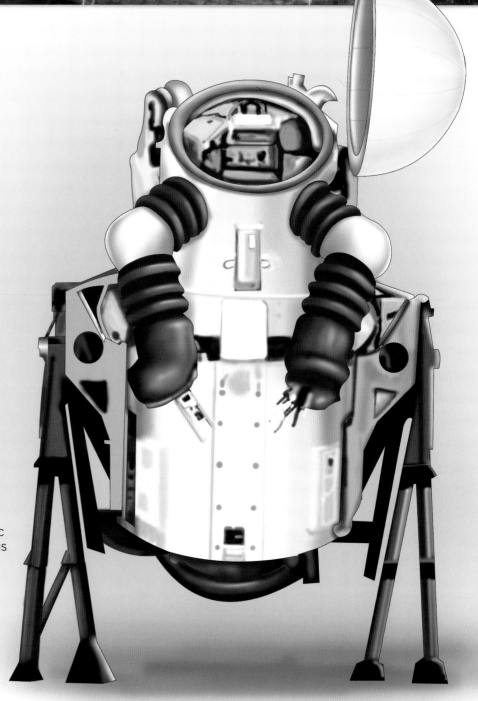

▶ *A robot submersible can help scientists in conducting underwater experiments*

AUTOSUB-1

▲ *The Autosub is an autonomous underwater vehicle (AUV) and is about 7m (23 ft) long*

LEGACIES AND LINERS!

Specially made passenger liners were a reality by the beginning of the 19th century. In 1818, a New York-based shipping company, Black Ball Line, introduced regular passenger services between America and England.

Cunard Comforts

The Cunard Line, founded in 1840 by Samuel Cunard, built some of the world's most famous liners. One of these, the *Queen Elizabeth* (1940), was the largest passenger ship of its time.

In the Lap of Luxury

By the 20th century, luxury travel had become the order of the day. In 1911, the first on-board health centre was built aboard the *Franconia*. A Cunard liner, *Aquitania*, housed the first ever indoor swimming pool on a ship. Soon there were squash courts and restaurants too. Modern-day liners like Norway's *The World* even offer full-fledged apartments for sale, complete with private balconies and jacuzzis!

▲ *Jacuzzi*

▼ *Sir Samuel Cunard (1787-1865)*

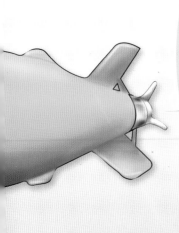

Which was the first ship to have an ice-skating rink and a miniature golf course?

The *Voyager of the Sea*, the largest liner in the world, was the first ship to have an ice-skating rink and a miniature golf course.

Who led the world's first successful voyage in a reed boat?

In the year 2000, Phil Buck, an American, led the world's first successful voyage in a reed boat. Going from Chile to Easter Island, he covered a distance of about 4,023 km (2,500 miles).

Which famous bridge in London parts to let tall ships pass through?

Tower Bridge is a bascule bridge, which makes way to let tall ships pass through. A French term, "bascule" means "see-saw".

What was the nickname for the Spanish Armada?

The Spaniards had believed that the Spanish Armada could never be defeated, and so they called it the "Invincible Armada". However, it was defeated by the English in 1588.

▲ *King Philip II of Spain had sent his great Armada to conquer England in 1588*

▼ *Tower Bridge was completed in 1894*

What is the age of the longest Viking ship?

The 36m (118 ft) long *Roskilde* 6, the longest Viking ship ever discovered, is believed to be over 970 years old.

Who holds the record for the fastest woman to sail around the world?

On February 11, 2001, Ellen MacArthur completed a solo voyage around the world, achieving the feat in just 94 days. She was aboard the *Kingfisher*.

Why were yachts invented?

The Dutch are said to have invented the yacht in the 17th century. Shipbuilders wanted to make faster and smaller ships that could evade pirates and safely transport goods to merchants. These ships were named "jachts", and soon became popular with the Dutch royalty for pleasure sailing.

FACT BOX

- In 1881, the Servia passenger cruise liner became the first ship to be lit by electricity.

- On July 30, 2001, David Leibowitz and Kimberley Miller, an American couple, got married in a tiny submarine resting on the remains of the Titanic!

- On August 11, 1989, the Japanese research submarine, *Shinkai 6500*, dived to a depth of 6,526 metres (21,411 ft). Until then, no other existing manned submarine had reached that depth.

▲ The Shinkai 6500 was launched in 1989, the very year it created the diving record!

◄ Propelled by either sail or engine, yachts are used for racing as well as recreation

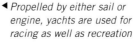

Who was the owner of the largest-ever junk?

Admiral Zheng He (pronounced Cheng Ho) owned the largest-ever junk – a flat-bottomed sailing vessel. Named after its owner, the *Zheng He* had nine masts and sailed the Chinese waters in the 1400's.

Who was the youngest survivor of the *Titanic* shipwreck?

The youngest *Titanic* survivor, Millvina Dean, was only nine weeks old when she escaped the shipwreck along with her mother and brother.

Where are the oldest preserved sails in the world?

The Vasa Museum, on the island of Djurgården in Sweden, houses the oldest preserved sails in the world. The sails belong to a Swedish warship, the *Vasa*, which sank on her first voyage in 1628.

▲ *The junk is a Chinese sailing craft dating back to ancient times*

How many boats were tied together to form the longest free-floating line in the world?

On June 25, 2000, 691 boats were tied together on Lake Norman, North Carolina, to form the longest free-floating line in the world.

When was the first on-board swimming pool built?

A swimming pool was first built aboard a ship in 1912. The ship was the celebrated *Titanic*, which was also the first to have a gymnasium on-board.

◄ *A swimming pool on the deck of a ship*

IN THE BEGINNING

The journey of trains began hundreds of years ago. References dating back to ancient times talk of vehicles being pulled along grooved, uneven roadways.

Wagons on Wheels

Miners in 16th-century Europe used the first known trains. These were wagons used to transport goods, and were called chaldrons. Later, horses were used for pulling loads uphill. The horses were then sent downhill in wagons called dandy carts. This was meant to save their energy!

Before Steam

Gradually, people started experimenting with vehicles that did not need to be pulled by horses or humans. However, it was the advent of the steam engine that really set the tale of trains on track. The first public steam railway for goods and passengers was the Liverpool and Manchester Railway in England, which opened in 1830.

When did the first known railways appear?

The first known railways appeared in the late 1700's, transporting goods such as coal over short distances. They had short trains of wagons connected to one another. These trains were pulled along by horses at the front.

Which is the oldest surviving station in the world?

The Liverpool Road Station in Manchester, U.K., is considered to be the world's oldest surviving station. It was opened in 1830.

What is unique about the *Puffing Billy*?

The *Puffing Billy* is one of the two oldest steam locomotives in existence. The other one is *Locomotion No. 1*. Built in 1813 by William Hedley, *Puffing Billy* is considered to be the first true train engine.

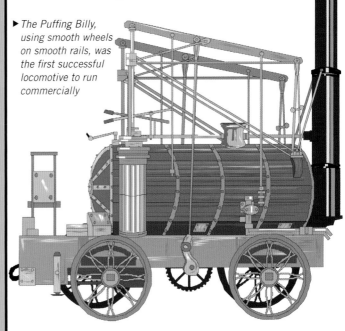

▶ *The Puffing Billy, using smooth wheels on smooth rails, was the first successful locomotive to run commercially*

What were wagonways?

As early as 1550, railed roads called wagonways were being used in Germany. These were made of wooden rails, over which horse-drawn wagons or carts moved.

◀ *The first-class carriages of the Liverpool and Manchester Railway were equipped with upholstered furniture and seats with armrests*

▼ *The advent of wagonways marked the beginnings of modern railways*

How was the speed of vehicles travelling downhill on wagonways controlled?

Loaded chaldrons, or wagons, were accompanied by a brakesman, who controlled the speed of the wagon by sitting on its handle, right behind the horse!

Why was Christmas Day in 1830 special for American railway history?

On December 25, 1830, America's first regular passenger train made its maiden voyage, from Charleston to Hamburg in South Carolina, U.S. The four-wheeled carriage was named *Best Friend of Charleston*.

What is the name of the world's first public steam railway line?

The world's first public railway to use steam was the Stockton and Darlington Railway in England. It was first opened for public use in 1825.

Which steam engine inspired the passenger train?

The Rocket steam engine, invented by an English engineer named Robert Stephenson, inspired the passenger train. Built in 1829, the Rocket was the first locomotive with modern rail features.

▼ *Best Friend of Charleston: America's first regular passenger train*

Which is the oldest train still in use?

The oldest surviving locomotive is the Fairy Queen. It was built in 1855 in England, for the East Indian Railways. Kept at the New Delhi Rail Museum in India, it is still used occasionally for running tourist trains.

Who invented the world's first self-propelled land vehicle?

In 1769, Frenchman Nicholas Cugnot built the first land vehicle to move by engine. The tractor-like locomotive was three-wheeled and one of the first attempts at steam locomotion.

▼ *Cugnot's steam engine was specially designed to run on common roads. It is preserved at the Museum of the Conservatoire des Arts et Metiers, in Paris, France*

FACT FILE

- In the early 1830's, it was common to find cows trespassing on American railroads. Isaac Dripps, a mechanical engineer in New Jersey, devised a solution to this problem. He fixed a bumper-like device on to the front of the locomotive. This device, which came to be known as the cowcatcher, helped in keeping cattle away and avoiding accidents.

- Station guards in the past signalled train drivers with the help of a rotatable oil lamp. The lamp contained glass that rotated to show green for "go" and red for "stop". The glass could also flash white for any other communication with drivers.

- The world's first regular passenger railway service was started in March 1807. The service was originally begun in 1806, though this was solely for transporting coal between Mumbles and Swansea in England.

How were railroad tracks laid in the past?

Earlier, railroad tracks were laid out by hand. The heavy rails had to be manually lifted and placed in their correct positions. Many workers were needed for this, since there were hardly any machines available then.

What were early track-laying workers also known as?

Workers who built railway lines were also known as navvies. The word "navvy" comes from "navigator". Navvies would dig the soil and build tracks using hand tools.

◄ *In the past, hand-held oil lamps were commonly used by station guards for signalling train drivers and track workers*

▼ *Early tracklayers used very basic equipment such as wheelbarrows, handpicks and shovels. Sometimes, railroad tracks took years to complete*

THE STORY CONTINUES

The story of railways would not have been, if it were not for steam!

Early Experiments
The steam vehicle that Cugnot built in 1769 was difficult to control and, therefore, unsafe. It was Richard Trevithick who came up with the first successful steam locomotive in 1804.

Stephenson's Steam
With his simple yet stable engines, George Stephenson took steam technology to new heights. Newer and better trains were built in America, Europe and Asia. Amongst these was the Novelty, one of the three entrants for the Liverpool and Manchester Railway trials. However, although the Novelty was the lightest and fastest engine, its boiler broke down too often.

Steaming Ahead
By the 1900's, cross-country travel led to improved passenger comfort and safety. The steam age had firmly paved the way for further innovations in railways.

▶ *The Novelty was built in six weeks by Ericsson and Braithwaite*

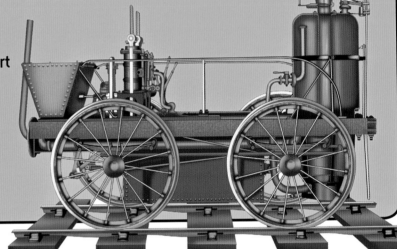

Who invented the steam engine?
In 1698, Thomas Savery built the first crude steam engine, which was based on Denis Papin's pressure cooker, the *Digester* (1679). Thomas Newcomen and James Watt later developed this engine further.

Why is Frank Julian Sprague an important personality in railway history?
Frank Julian Sprague was an American electrical engineer who helped develop the first practical city trolley system, the modern subway, elevated trains and automatic safety controls for trains.

What were Orphan Trains?
During 1854 to 1930, up to 200,000 orphans, street children and runaways were transported from eastern U.S. to the western states, being sent to foster families. The trains carrying them were called Orphan Trains, Baby Trains, or Mercy Trains.

When were sleeper cars invented?
In 1857, George Pullman invented sleeper cars for overnight passenger travel. The first Pullman sleeper, the Pioneer, was attached to the funeral train carrying Abraham Lincoln's body in 1865.

▼ *Pullman sleepers are believed to have been the world's first fully electrically lit and steam-heated cars*

Did anyone ever invent a train that ran on water?

One of the unusual inventions in the late 1800's included hydraulic, or water, trains, also called sliding railways. M. Girard's 1868 sliding railway and the Barre Sliding Railway were two such innovations. The latter had carriages that propelled themselves along watered tracks. The ride was created for the 1876 Chicago World's Fair.

Why is Frank Julian Sprague an important personality in railway history?

Frank Julian Sprague was an American electrical engineer who helped develop the first practical city trolley system, the modern subway, elevated trains and automatic safety controls for trains.

How did the Julian system of electrically lit trains work?

Julian Sprague devised electrical batteries that could be placed in compartments below, and along the sides of, the carriages of a train. These batteries were connected to the interiors of the train through circuits, providing light to the switches and lamps in cabins.

▼ Early hydraulic trains like the Barre Sliding Railway had no wheels and ran on water

▼ The Julian electric battery

Who were the "Big Boys"?

The "Big Boys" were actually locomotives built in 1941-44 for the Union Pacific Railroad, and were so called because they were among the largest steam locomotives ever to be built!

What are diesel-electric trains?

Diesel-electric trains are powered both by generators and diesel engines. Diesel trains are considered to be more environmentally friendly and easier to maintain than steam trains. By the 1950's, steam-powered trains were displaced by diesel and electric locomotives.

Who invented the first electric train?

German inventor Werner von Siemens built the world's first electric train in 1879. For the first time, a locomotive was powered by a generator. The world's first electrified railway was opened in Germany in 1881.

What kinds of jobs did early railway porters do?

Early porters would receive passengers and transport their luggage to the train. It was also their job to make up the cabins, and serve food and drinks to passengers.

▼ *Early railway porters waited at station platforms with luggage trolleys, to help passengers with luggage*

FACT FILE

- During World War I, a shortage of workers led the United Railways and Electric Company to hire women, for the first time, as train conductors.

- In the past, passengers at small stations used to stop trains by waving a "tin flag". This was a round tin plate attached to a pole. Trains would stop only if the passenger on the platform waved this flag!

- At first, trains ran only during the day, and railway headlights did not exist. Later, as trains began to operate at night, people thought of different ways to light up the tracks ahead. These included experiments with bonfires, candles and reflectors in glass cases and kerosene lamps. Eventually, gas lights became common, followed by electric lights in 1881.

◄ *Early train headlight*

When were major railway tunnels built?

Trains sometimes needed to pass through mountains, so tunnels started to be built in the 19th century. The Simplon Tunnel (1898-1906) between Iselle, Italy, and Brig, Switzerland, is almost 20 km (12 miles) long!

Which inventor is commonly regarded as the "Father of Railways"?

George Stephenson is commonly hailed as the "Father of Railways". His inventions include the first steam locomotive and the Blucher: a locomotive that could pull 30,000 kg (66,138 lbs) up a hill at 6 kph (4 mph).

▶ *George Stephenson was the first person to use steam for powering locomotives, paving the way for faster and more efficient railway travel*

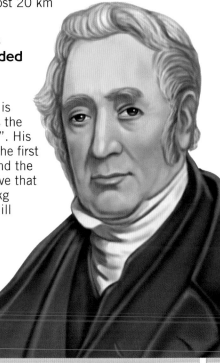

TRAIN TYPES

From the first wagonways to high-speed passenger trains – all kinds of trains have been invented over the years.

Locomotive Language

Although steam trains can still be seen in many places, electric trains are now more common in big cities. Diesel trains are popular too.

Tunnel Trains

As cities became crowded, more trains were needed. There was little space for them, though. The solution was underground trains. Indeed, they have made day-to-day travel so fast and easy!

Tilting Technology

Advances in technology have led to the development of such high-tech, high-speed trains as tilting trains. They are designed to tilt to one side. Italy's ETR 450 Pendolino is a famous tilting train.

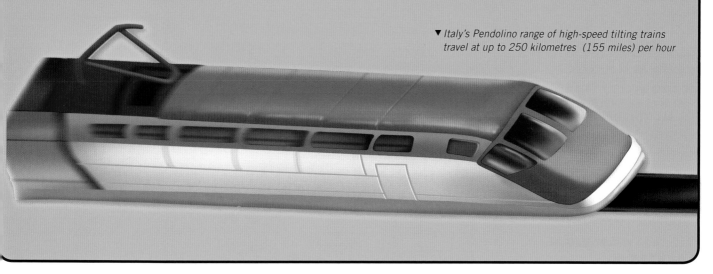

▼ *Italy's Pendolino range of high-speed tilting trains travel at up to 250 kilometres (155 miles) per hour*

◄ *Double-decker trains are popular because they save space, while accommodating more people*

What are the two basic types of trains?

There are two types of trains – passenger trains for carrying people from one place to another, and freight trains, which are designed specially to carry goods in big boxes, or containers.

Are there trains that look like double-decker buses?

Some railway lines, such as Amtrak in the United States, manufacture double-deck trains for long-distance travel. These Amtrak superliners are usually 26m (85 ft) long. Their coaches carry over 70 passengers, on two levels, with storage space for luggage on the lower level.

What are the different types of rail cars?

The different kinds of rail cars include: Amtrak Superliners, open-top hopper cars, covered hopper cars, double-stack container cars, tank cars, gondola cars, enclosed rack cars, boxcars, piggy-bank cars, refrigerator cars, centre-beam cars and cabooses.

▲ Auto racks are specially designed to transport vehicles. They usually have two or three levels. Triple-deck auto racks carry automobiles, while vans and trucks are transported in double-deck racks

Which kind of rail cars can carry as many as 18 automobiles?

Enclosed autorack cars have two or three enclosed decks for transporting vehicles. They can hold about 18 automobiles.

What are subways?

Underground railways in North America are called subways. The New York City subway consists of as many as 277 underground stations!

What is an underground railway system?

An underground railway system functions in tunnels below the ground. They are useful in busy cities because they avoid traffic jams and also travel across large distances quickly.

Which rail car carries vegetables and fruits?

Refrigerator cars carry both fresh and frozen fruits, vegetables and meat. About 18m (60 ft) long, they have a system – similar to that of conventional refrigerators – for preserving food products.

▶ Gondola cars are open freight cars that usually have low and flat-bottomed sides

FACT FILE

● There are three kinds of underground railways – open-cut, cut-and-cover, and tube. In an open-cut type, streets are torn out to build railways in ditches. When there is a pavement over the cut, it is called cut-and-cover; while the tube is built by boring through the earth.

● Piggyback cars are freight cars that carry containers, one on top of the other. They are flatcars fixed with a device that can usually carry two containers. Piggyback cars are also called huckepack carriages.

● Gondola cars got their name from their gondola-like shape. They can be open or covered, and carry metal products and bulk freight. They are usually 16m (53 ft) long.

What kind of trains can lean to the side to increase speed?

Tilting trains can actually tilt to the side in order to increase speed. One of the first such trains was the Deutsche Bahn AG. However, tilting trains did not initially take off because many passengers complained of feeling sick due to sudden tilting movements!

How do trains help to transport animals from one place to another?

Livestock rail cars are used to transport animals, like cows, sheep and horses, over long distances.

What is a monorail?

A monorail is a single rail track for passenger or freight vehicles. The first passenger-carrying monorail, the Cheshunt Railway, opened in 1825. It was built to carry bricks, but created history by carrying passengers instead!

Which is the oldest underground railway line?

The oldest underground railway is the Metropolitan Railway in London. It began operations in 1863 with the opening of its first section – between the stations Paddington and Farringdon.

How is a commuter train different from an intercity train?

Commuter trains are passenger trains that carry people within large cities, like London and New York, and between nearby areas. Intercity trains move from one city to another.

◄ *The most modern tilting trains are no longer uncomfortable for passengers, as they are now built with more advanced technology*

▼ *A livestock freight car*

▼ *The first commercial monorail service opened in Germany in 1901. Today, monorail systems are present in many countries*

TRAIN TALK

Train locomotion technology began with steam, later developing to include diesel and electricity.

▶ Trains are sometimes signalled with coloured flags when the usual electric systems of signalling are not working

The Era of Engines

Steam engines have a fire box, which is filled with hot coal. The coal heats the water boiler in the engine, and the heated water takes the form of steam. The steam moves an instrument called a piston, which, in turn, moves the wheels.

Tracks and Technology

If it weren't for railway lines, equipment and networking, train technology would not have progressed as much. Previously, track-laying had been a hard task, involving many workers and lots of time. Over time, better rails, wheels and gauges led to safer and smoother travel. Later, tracks on bridges, mountains and underground followed. Signalling systems evolved, from hand signs and flagging, to computerised electric lights. Today, railway networks the world and are well-organised and efficient.

What is a railway?

A railway is made up of a track, along which locomotives pull trains of cars. It also includes signal systems to control train traffic, and stations to handle passengers and goods.

▶ All railway lines have signals along the tracks for the smooth functioning of railway networks

What are signal boxes?

Signal boxes are towers or buildings that contain equipment for signalling and switching the track configuration. Early signal boxes had manual equipment, with an attendant to control them. Modern-day signal centres are computerised.

How do electric currents in overhead wires reach an electric train?

Most electric trains are connected to overhead power lines by a pantograph. The arm-like pantograph gathers electric currents from the powered wires and transports the currents to the driving motors of the train.

▼ An early signal box

How are electric locomotives different from diesel-electric locomotives?

Diesel locomotives carry their generators on-board. Electric locomotives, on the other hand, receive power supply from external generating centres through overhead wires or charged rails.

What kinds of railway signals are used to guide train drivers?

In the 1800's, railway policemen would signal to drivers with colourful flags and batons. Later, signals became mechanical. The 1920's saw the introduction of coloured lights for trains. Nowadays, automatic semaphore signals help maintain safety at level crossings and stations.

What is the difference between a locomotive and a train?

A locomotive is a machine that moves the train on railway tracks. Locomotives are of three types – diesel, electric and steam.

Who invented the refrigeration system for trains?

Fred McKinley Jones invented an automatic refrigeration system for long-haul trucks in 1935. It helped to reduce the risk of food spoilage during long-distance trips.

How is a train route built?

First, the land is levelled. This is called grading. Then, the route is covered with gravel and crushed stone, also called ballasts. This helps to drain rainwater and avoid the growth of weeds.

▼ *Automatic railway crossing gates control the movement of trains running through busy streets*

FACT FILE

▼ *The invention of flanged wheels made train travel safer, minimising possibilities of derailment*

- Railway tracks are made of metals, which usually stretch with increasing temperature, and contract with decreasing temperature. If tracks are made without gaps, the metal will keep stretching and shrinking, which could lead to disasters.

- The distance between two running rails is called a railway gauge. Gauges are different for different countries. For example, it is one metre for East Africa, while in Japan, it is 1.067 metres.

- Trains use wheels that have a flange around the inner edge. A flange is a raised inside edge, which keeps the wheels on track and guides the cart around curves. Flanged wheels keep trolleys on track and reduce friction, which allows for easier movement.

Can railway tracks be switched or moved?

Railway tracks comprise of continuous welded rails that help trains to run smoothly. Switches or points at the criss-cross sections in the rails move the trains to different sections of the track. The track-switching is done from signal boxes or towers with the help of switching levers. In the past, it was common to switch the tracks manually, which was done by pulling levers.

◀ *Small stations in many countries still use the manual system of changing tracks. Levers on the side of the tracks, or inside signal boxes, are operated to guide trains onto, or off, specific routes*

Who invented automatic air brakes?

George Westinghouse invented a system of air brakes in 1868. These air brakes went a long way in making train travel safe.

How is a rail car different from a train?

Rail cars are self-powered vehicles with a built-in power unit. They generate their own power and are not supported by a locomotive. Trains, however, need locomotive power to run.

How do drivers keep track of faults on the train, or any dangers ahead?

A train driver's cab is equipped with several gadgets and controls. These allow the driver to drive the train safely. Radio communication also enables the driver to keep in touch with signalling centres, so that there are no train collisions.

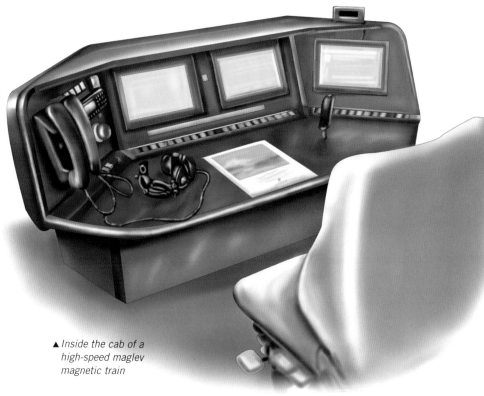

▲ *Inside the cab of a high-speed maglev magnetic train*

TRAINS WITH A DIFFERENCE

Among the hundreds of different trains that have been built, some stand out as unique, being specially designed for specific purposes.

Trains with Tasks

In the past, there were circus trains that carried circus animals and performers. Ski trains took skiers to snowy slopes. In 1939, a train in Canada was converted into a travelling dental clinic! In the 1900's, Canadian children who lived too far to go to school everyday had their schools come to them on-board trains: the cars were divided into classrooms and living quarters for teachers!

In places that receive a lot of snowfall, special trains clear snow off the tracks. In earthquake-prone Japan, special equipment warns Bullet Train drivers about tremors and storms beforehand.

Funicular Fun

Funiculars are short-length railways meant specially for uphill travel. These run on stationary engines, and consist of two short trains joined by a steel cable. The world's first funicular train, La Ficelle, was probably launched in 1877.

Who built the Railplane?

George Bennie, an engineer, invented the Railplane in 1930. The Railplane was a suspended, monorail-like vehicle that ran along rails using a propeller. Bennie tried to combine the technologies used in making aeroplanes and trains.

How are suspended monorails different from ordinary monorails?

Suspended monorails consist of trains that run under the track, suspended from above. Ordinary monorails run on top of a single track, rather than under it.

How fast was the *Hiawatha*?

The *Hiawatha* was a steam-powered passenger train built to run at high speeds. Launched in 1935, it travelled from Chicago to Minneapolis-St. Paul, U.S., in just 5 hours and 5 minutes.

▼ *Funicular trains run on normal rails, with an extra cogged rail in the centre that pulls the train uphill and keeps it from sliding downhill*

What are ICE trains?

ICE is the name for Germany's Inter City Express trains. They provide for air-conditioned, noiseless and speedy travel. Glass panels separate the front carriages of these trains, giving a clear view of the driver's cab. ICE trains are equipped with various comforts like restaurants, lounges, incoming telephone facilities and reclining seats.

What kind of a train is the Lifeline Express?

The Lifeline Express in India is the world's first complete hospital on rails. It consists of three air-conditioned carriages that house an operating theatre, ward rooms and a sterilisation room. The "hospital" also has living cabins for the medical crew.

What is the People Mover?

The People Mover is an automatic railcar that usually runs on an elevated, single-track loop. It operates in small, specific areas such as parts of towns, or at resorts, airports and amusement centres.

Which was the first train to travel on a cushion of air?

The Aerotrain was the first train built to travel on a cushion of air. It was built by Frenchman Jean Bertin in the early 1960's.

▲ ICE trains are the fastest land vehicles in Germany, with a speed of nearly 300 kph (186 mph)

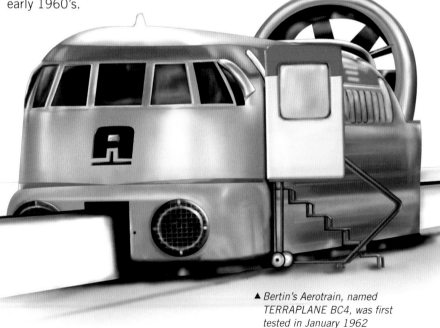

▲ Bertin's Aerotrain, named TERRAPLANE BC4, was first tested in January 1962

FACT FILE

- In the late 1800's, special trains called Silk Trains carried raw silk from Vancouver, Canada, to silk mills in New York and New Jersey, U.S. These trains, worth over two million dollars each, were accompanied by armed security guards!

- Alaska is home to the Fish Train, the only train in the world used solely for transporting raw fish! It is known as the Yakutat and Southern Railroad.

- The world's fastest conventional passenger train is France's Train à Grande Vitesse (TGV). It travels between Paris and Lyon. Its top speed of about 515 kph (320 mph) is about half the speed of sound!

▲ *The world's fastest conventional train was aptly named Train á Grande Vitesse, which means "high-speed train" in French*

Which is only the second railway to be declared a UNESCO World Heritage site?

India's Darjeeling Himalayan Railway is the world's second railway to receive a World Heritage site status, following the first one in Australia. Popularly called the *Darjeeling Toy Train*, the tiny train journeys up the foothills of the Himalayas to Ghoom, the second highest railway station in the world!

◄ *Over 100 years old, the Darjeeling Toy Train takes tourists on a scenic 86 km (53 mile) long ride, lasting about six hours*

Where can you find the world's first train to be run without a driver?

The first driverless train in the world is based in Vancouver, Canada. Known as the Vancouver Skytrain, it was introduced in 1986.

Is the *Flying Hamburger* really a train?

The 1933 *Flying Hamburger* was a high-speed diesel railcar introduced in Germany. It ran between Berlin and Hamburg at a speed of 161 kph (100 mph).

Why is the Standing Train of Japan so called?

The Standing Train of Japan is so called because it does not have any seats! Passengers on the train lean against a steel bar, which runs through the middle of each of its carriages.

Which is the fastest locomotive in the world?

In 1938, Mallard became the fastest steam locomotive in the world. It clocked a maximum speed of 203 kph (126 mph).

▶ *The Mallard was built in 1938 by Sir Nigel Gresley, a British engineer*

RAILWAY ROUTES AND STATIONS

What did early stations look like? How were routes and networks developed to connect cities and nations?

Railway Routes

The popularity of trains led to more and more railway routes – over rivers, up mountains, and under the ground. Thanks to the invention of sleeper cars, electric lighting and dining cars, long-distance travel was finally possible. A new era for train stations had begun!

Station Speak

Modern railway stations are equipped with easy-to-use ticket machines that can be operated by passengers at any time of the day or night. Early train stations were wooden sheds alongside railway tracks. Some did not even have platforms. Modern stations are very different though, housing nearly everything a passenger needs – from automatic ticket machines to vending machines for food and drinks, restrooms and shops. In Japan, many stations even have hot springs in the vicinity for people to relax in, before and after journeying!

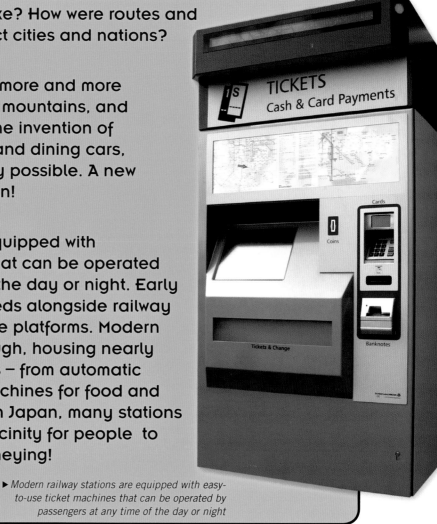

▶ Modern railway stations are equipped with easy-to-use ticket machines that can be operated by passengers at any time of the day or night

What is the name of Britain's longest railway tunnel?

The longest train tunnel in Britain is known as the Severn Tunnel. It stretches for 7 km (4.5 miles), and is said to take more than two hours to walk through!

▼ Train tunnels are built so that they are slightly broader than the gauge of the tracks, to enable a train to make an easy passage

What is special about the Peruvian Central Railway?

The Peruvian Central Railway is the highest railway in the world. It climbs 3,962m (13,000 feet) on its trip from La Oroya to Lima, Peru. The railroad features 66 tunnels and 59 bridges, and zigzags across valleys. There is an on-board doctor for giving oxygen to passengers who get height sickness!

How large is the world's largest continuous railway route?

The Trans-Siberian Express in Russia is the world's largest continuous railway, covering 9, 300 km (5, 778 miles) and making 91 stops in 9 days. It runs between Moscow and Vladivostok, making for the longest regular train trip in the world.

What is the latest PIE system built for railway stations?

The Information and Emergency Point (PIE) is a computer that combines voice and video assistance for emergencies or just general information. The PIE is set in a metal cupboard, which is made of vandal-proof material and anti-graffiti paint!

▶ Hi-tech gadgets for passenger convenience, such as the Information and Emergency Point (PIE), are becoming increasingly common at railway stations today

▲ *An interior view of New York's Grand Central Terminal railway station*

Which is the largest railway station in the world?

The Grand Central Terminal in the United States is the largest railway station in the world. It has 44 platforms.

Was there a railway that journeyed to the top of a volcano?

In 1880, a funicular railway was built to go to the top of Italy's Mount Vesuvius. It was the only railway to ascend to the summit of a volcano.

Which is the longest monorail in the world?

The Osaka Monorail in Japan is the world's longest monorail. It stretches over a length of 22 km (14 miles), running between Osaka International Airport and the Hankyu and Keihan railway stations.

▶ *London Underground's famous logo, as we know it today, was designed in 1913 by Edward Johnston*

FACT FILE

● The world's longest stretch of straight railway track helps connect the cities of Sydney and Perth in Australia. The route, opened in 1970, is 478 km (297 miles) in length!

● The oldest station in the London Underground network is Baker Street Station, famous for its association with the fictional detective, Sherlock Holmes! With over 400 km (248.5 miles) of track, London Underground is the longest underground railway network in the world.

The Liverpool Road station in Manchester, England, is now a part of the Museum of Science and Industry.

When did the Eurostar begin to run?

The Eurostar was opened in 1994. It linked the capital cities of France (Paris), Belgium (Brussels) and England (London) through the English Channel. The Eurotunnel project included a dual rail tunnel for trains and shuttles carrying motor vehicles.

Which is the largest railway network in the world?

Indian Railways is the largest railway network in the world. It caters to over 10 million people, with 11,000 trains running daily.

Why is the Shanghai South Railway station unique?

The Shanghai South Railway is the world's first round station. It is shaped like a wheel, and has a transparent roof. The waiting room has space for about 10,000 people.

Where is the world's longest station seat located?

England's Scarborough Station is home to the longest station seat in the world. It is nearly 140m (459 ft) long.

Which famous train journey connects two oceans?

The Indian Pacific train covers one of the world's longest straight railway tracks, measuring 478 km (293 miles). It connects two oceans while travelling from Sydney to Perth. It even offers an off-train sightseeing tour, during which one may spot the Australian wedge-tailed eagle, the symbol of the train.

▲ *Eurostar is the fastest passenger train service in the United Kingdom, carrying over seven million passengers each year*

▼ *The route taken by the Indian Pacific, from Sydney to Perth, covers 4,352 km (2,704 miles)*

TRAMS AND TROLLEYS

An older form of the train, trams are an important part of railway heritage. These are light-rail passenger vehicles for short-distance travel, running along rails laid in the middle of streets. While the early trams were usually pulled along by horses, the modern ones move by means of overhead electric cables.

Around the World

Tramways are still common in places such as Switzerland, Austria, Poland, France, Australia, India and Hong Kong. In the United States, most trams had disappeared by the mid-1900's. However, the cable cars of San Francisco remain amongst the most famous in the world.

▲ The famous vintage trams of San Francisco are more than a 100 years old

What were Motormanettes?

It is believed that during the early 1900's, the town of Venice in California, U.S., ran trackless, bench-like trams called motormanettes. These were ran on electric battery. Uniformed motormen would operate the hand levers and mechanical brakes at the ends of the vehicle!

▼ Motormanettes were once operated between Santa Monica and Venice in the United States

How did trams originate?

The first horse-drawn buses were used in 1829. However, the roads were so bad that the wheels of these buses constantly got stuck in mud or potholes. In the 1860's, iron rails along the roads made travelling less bumpy, thus paving the way for horse-drawn trams.

Were early trams drawn by animals other than horses?

Mules were often used by street railway services to pull railcars carrying both passengers and goods. The Seguin Street Railway in Texas was known to run mule-drawn railcars in the 1900's.

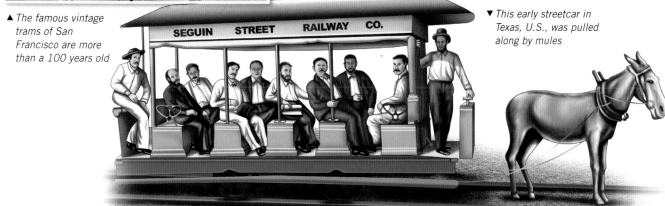

▼ This early streetcar in Texas, U.S., was pulled along by mules

What are double-width trams?

Double-width trams have cushions of air under them, which allow them to glide on smooth road surfaces. The trams have tracking wheels on the sides connecting them to the cables fitted on the edges of double-width tracks. In this way, two different trams can move on the opposite sides of the same track!

Where is the oldest commercial tram service located?

The world's oldest tramway that still charges for rides is the Manx Electric Railway (MER). It is located on the Isle of Man in the United Kingdom, and was opened in September 1893.

Why was it a bad idea to have open-top roofs on double-decker steam trams?

The first double-decker steam trams were designed with open rooftops. However, the steam and cinders coming out of the tram chimney often set fire to the top hats of the gentlemen passengers below!

Which is the oldest street railway line?

The oldest street railway line is the 1835 New Orleans and Carrollton line. It continues to operate along the route now known as the St. Charles Streetcar line.

◄ The advanced double-width tram at the Getty Center in America

▼ A railcar

FACT FILE

- In 1885, Fleetwood became the first town in the United Kingdom to use electric trams.

- The first tramway in New York was established in 1832. Located in Manhattan, it was drawn by two horses and could seat nearly 50 passengers.

- Railcars usually have one or more coaches attached together and a driver's cab at each end.

What is special about the Chesterfield Tram 7 at the National Tramway Museum?

The Chesterfield Tram 7 was used as a holiday home after the Chesterfield Corporation Tramways shut down. Its upper and lower decks were separated and placed alongside each other as a living room and a bedroom! Visitors to the National Tramway Museum in Crich, England, can now enjoy rides on the restored tram.

What makes trams environmentally friendly?

Trams run on electricity, so they do not give out fumes and pollute the environment. They are also good for the environment because they move quietly on smooth rails, without causing noise pollution.

Why are the trams of Strasbourg in France famous?

Strasbourg's modern trams are the first in France to have low-level floors. This makes the trams more suitable for elderly people and those with disabilities. Launched in 1994, the new-age trams are also famous for their sleek and modern design as well as high efficiency.

▼ The Chesterfield Tram

CHESTERFIELD CORPORATION TRAMWAYS

TO ERAMPTON

Which famous singer bought a tram to display in his garden?

Sir Elton John is said to have bought a classic W2 tram (No. 520) in Melbourne, Australia. He had it shipped back to his residence in Windsor, England, where it is displayed in the garden.

When did the first electric tram start operating?

The first electric tram in the world started operating in May 1881, on the Gross-Lichterfelde tracks in Berlin, Germany. The tram was built by the Siemens company.

◄ Modern trams like this one in Strasbourg, France, are nothing like the simple, wooden street carriages of the early days

The tale of trains would be incomplete without remembering those legendary figures whose unusual deeds earned them a place in railway history.

Historic Heroes

Take train conductor Harriet Tubman, for instance. In the mid-1800's, over a 10 year period, she helped some 300 slaves escape through the Underground Railroad network.

The Great Train Robbers

Then there were others who became known for their daring train thefts, which were common in the 19th century. Some famous train robbers were Jesse James, Bruce Reynolds and Butch Cassidy.

William Pierce was the mastermind behind the famous theft in 1855 of gold bars worth £12,000 from a train. The bars were being taken to the Crimean War site to pay British troops.

▼ The Great Train Robbery of 1855 was unprecedented in terms of the amount stolen

How is the phrase "hands up" related to trains?

The famous phrase "hands up" was supposedly first used by train robber Bill Miner, also known as the Gentleman Bandit. He said the words while robbing a Canadian Pacific Railways train in 1904, at Mission Junction, British Columbia.

What is unusual about the Swiss Federal Railway's *Re 482* locomotive?

The *Re 482* electric locomotive is a cargo train that was specially made to run on both the German and Swiss railway networks.

▼ Switzerland's Re 482 Cargo Locomotive

Which is the biggest railway tunnel in the world?

The Seikan Tonneru Tunnel in Japan is the world's biggest railway tunnel. It measures nearly 54 km (33.5 miles) in length. The tunnel was constructed between 1964 & 1988. The digging required 3,000 workers at any one time!

How are underground tunnels cleaned?

Underground tunnels are cleaned using various methods. The Paris metro, for instance, has a machine called the Cleaning Robot. Its large fan blows the dirt off the walls, while a vacuum cleaner sucks it up.

Which train and railway station were the inspiration behind the phrase "red-carpet treatment"?

A red carpet at New York's Grand Central Terminal led to the entrance of the luxury train, Twentieth Century Ltd. This is where the common phrase, "red-carpet treatment," originated!

▼ *The 20th Century Limited made its first journey in 1902, from New York to Chicago, U.S.*

What makes the Bullet Train of Japan so fast?

The bullet-like shape of the Bullet Train allows it to travel at up to 210 kph (130 mph). This high-speed train's original route was started between the Japanese cities of Osaka and Tokyo.

▼ *Japan's Bullet Train is also known as the Shinkansen. It is one of the fastest trains in the world*

Why was a race held between the Tom Thumb locomotive and a horse?

In 1830, a famous race was held between a horse and the steam locomotive Tom Thumb. Peter Cooper, the manufacturer of the locomotive, wanted to convince Baltimore and Ohio Railroad officials to use locomotives, rather than horses, to pull trains.

Do a train's crew members have a separate living space in the train?

Conductors and other staff members stay in cabooses, which are usually at the rear of the train. Cabooses serve as offices as well as living quarters for the crew members.

▼ Caboose cars are also sometimes called crummies, cabins, or hacks

How did Amtrak Railways get its name?

Amtrak, the United States's official railway service, got its name by blending together the words "American" and "track". Amtrak serves more than 500 stations in 46 states.

Which old train had an on-board hair-dressing salon and a cinema?

The Flying Scotsman – running between London's King's Cross station and Edinburgh, Scotland, until 1963 – was a luxury express train with a hair-dressing salon, a restaurant and bar, and a cinema coach.

Why did a worker ride on the engine of every steam train of the Mumbles Railway Line in England?

Every steam train of the Mumbles Railway Service had a man riding on its engine. It was his job to signal a bell in case of any danger signs on the tracks ahead! Two rings of the bell would warn the driver to hit the train's brakes.

How does the ventilation system in underground railways work?

Underground railways are built so that there is a proper ventilation of fresh air to breathe. Stale air is carried out through vents, while fresh air comes in by means of fans.

▶ The Flying Scotsman was the first non-stop train from London, England, to Edinburgh, Scotland

Passenger comforts were introduced early in railway history. By the mid-1800's, most European and American trains had toilets, lighting, heating and catering facilities.

Wealth on Wheels

In 1865, George Pullman introduced the world's first luxury trains. These had special dining cars, chandeliers, silk-shaded lamps and leather seats. South Africa's modern-day Rovos Rail is said to have the most spacious deluxe and royal suites.

Royal Ride

Royalty has always been provided with the best of comforts. The first royal train journey took place over 150 years ago. Some early royal trains, like Queen Victoria, had special royal stations too.

Later, royal trains were done up with plush interiors. There was a special daytime saloon for the Queen, and a smoking compartment for the King!

▲ With an area of 16 sq m (172 sq ft), each royal suite on the Rovos Rail takes up half of one carriage and includes a private lounge area and a bathroom with a Victorian bath

What did the head-lamps on the engines of royal trains look like?

The head-lamps of royal train engines were usually decorated with coats of arms or other signs of royalty.

▼ The ornate head-lamp of the Royal Gladstone

Why is the royal carriage of Queen Adelaide special?

Queen Adelaide's Carriage was the first-known royal saloon. Made in 1842, it was designed to look like a stagecoach.

▼ *Queen Adelaide's Carriage – the world's first royal saloon coach*

What kinds of food and drink are served abroad the British Luxury train, *Northern Belle*?

Multi-course meals aboard the lavish *Northern Belle* include freshly prepared gourmet food like Scottish beef fillet, potato rosti and mushrooms, a variety of cheeses and rich desserts. Fine wines and champagne are served in sparkling crystal glasses.

◄ *The dining cars of the Northern Belle are named and themed after British stately homes and castles. They are divided into two-or-four-seaters, each with a large table*

Which royal train was pulled by the steam locomotive *Phoenix*?

The 1863 *Phoenix* pulled the royal train of Bavaria's King Ludwig II. The train had one open-terrace car and one enclosed carriage. Its interiors were decorated with navy-blue velvet furniture and gold.

Which cities were linked by the Orient-Express?

The Orient-Express, also known as the Simplon-Orient-Express, linked the cities of London, Paris, Bucharest, Istanbul and Vienna. The train was famous for its five-course French meals and important passengers, who included diplomats, royalty and government couriers.

Which famous novel's title was inspired by the Orient Express?

Agatha Christie's *Murder on the Orient Express* was set on the Simplon-Orient-Express.

FACT FILE

- The *Queen of Scots* luxury train has the oldest railway dining car in the world. Built in 1890, it can seat 12 people.

- The *Royal Scotsman* has often been called a "country house hotel on wheels". Passengers are greeted by a bagpiper player in traditional kilt. The train maintains its Scottish Highlands charm inside too, with tartan-themed furniture and cuisine. For after-dinner entertainment, there is Scottish fiddle music and dancing.

- The Midnight Sun Express in Alaska is the only train to have an open-air viewing platform and its own gift shop.

What kind of train was the *Golden Arrow*?

The *Golden Arrow* was the name for the famous luxury train-and-ferry service that operated between London and Paris. It started running in 1929. It would stop at Dover, England, where passengers would get on to a ferry to cross the English Channel to Calais, France.

▶ *The regal logo of the Royal Scotsman luxury train*

GREAT SCOTT & WESTERN RAILWAY CO

THE ROYAL SCOTSMAN

Where can you find the only glass-domed, double-decker transcontinental train?

The United States is home to the *Santa Fe Express - Grand Luxe*, the world's only glass-domed, double-deck transcontinental luxury train. All the carriages have glass covers, so that passengers can even "sleep under the stars"!

Which luxury train had an on-board barbershop?

The *Twentieth Century Ltd.* housed its own barbershop. It was a luxury train connecting New York and Chicago during 1902-67.

Is the *Blue Train* really blue?

The Blue Train, often called "a five-star hotel on wheels", runs between Pretoria and Cape Town in South Africa. It gets its name from its blue locomotives, railcars and leather seats. All its suites have televisions and phones.

Who was the first royal figure to travel by train?

Queen Victoria became the first monarch to travel by train. Her journey from Slough to Paddington, England, took place in 1842.

Where is the Palace on Wheels?

The *Palace on Wheels* is a luxury train in India. It takes people across the state of Rajasthan and the cities of New Delhi and Agra. This 14-carriage train has been rated amongst the world's 10 best luxurious trains.

▲ *Passengers get a breathtaking view from the cars of the Santa Fe Express - Grand Luxe*

▼ *Suites on the Blue Train are elaborately decorated and fitted with the best and latest of comforts*

All over the world, people are proud of their history. There are museums to showcase this history, freezing time for future generations to see. Thus, there are special museums for preserving a nation's railway heritage, too.

Matchless Museums

National railway museums are usually a country's official museum for railways. The National Railway Museum in York, England, is the world's largest museum of its type. It houses over 100 locomotives, 3,000 models and more than 7,000 posters!

Some museums focus on special trains. The Model Train Museum in Canada has the world's largest collection of model and toy trains on display.

Ageless Artefacts

Railway museums house timeless treasures that take visitors back in time. Displays include replica models of engines and trains, signalling gear, track-laying tools, uniforms, tickets and crockery. Some museums have special rooms showcasing toy trains and various paintings and illustrations on the railways and luxury saloon cars.

Where is the biggest collection of model railway vehicles made by one person?

The largest set of model train vehicles made by one individual is the J.P. Richards Collection. It is situated at England's National Railway Museum in York, which is also home to the world's largest collection of railway icons. James Peel Richards made all 610 models in the collection by hand.

How were long-distance trains stocked up with extra supplies of water?

Water carriers preserved at some railway museums show that long-distance trains were given extra water supplies at stations. Water-filling carriers were wheeled on to the platform, and by means of a hose connected to the train's dining car, provided a refill of drinking water.

Where can you see enactments of old train robberies?

At most railway heritage sites and museums in the United States, historic train robberies are acted out for visitors. The Grand Canyon Railway recreates train robberies of the early 1900's, along a 105 km (65 mile) journey in an original 1923 Pullman Coach!

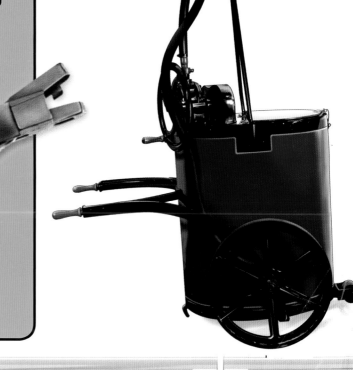

▶ Water carriers were connected by hosepipe to trains for re-filling the train's lavatory and dining car water tanks

▲ Early railway collectors used these punchers to check tickets

What were the "tea and sugar" trains?

In 1918, vans carrying tea, sugar, flour, boiled beef, cabbage, salt and pepper, and rice were run for supplying provisions to railway-track workers constructing the 1,693 km (1,052 mile) long Trans-Australian Railway.

What did the whistles of early station guards look like?

Early station guards and staff members had simple metal or wooden whistles to communicate with each other. These whistles were also used to inform train drivers when to leave the station. Most railway museums have such whistles on display.

▲ Small metal whistles served as a means of communication for early railway staff members

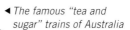

◄ The famous "tea and sugar" trains of Australia

Which American museum houses exhibits from the "trolley era"?

The Connecticut Trolley Museum – founded in October 1940 and owned by the Railway Association, Inc. – has exhibits from the "trolley era", the period in New England between 1890 and 1945.

What is special about the wheels displayed outside the National Rail Museum in York, England?

The wheels on display outside the National Rail Museum in York are said to be the largest existing steam locomotive wheels. They were the central wheels of a locomotive belonging to the Bristol and Exeter Railways.

▼ The world's largest steam locomotive wheels

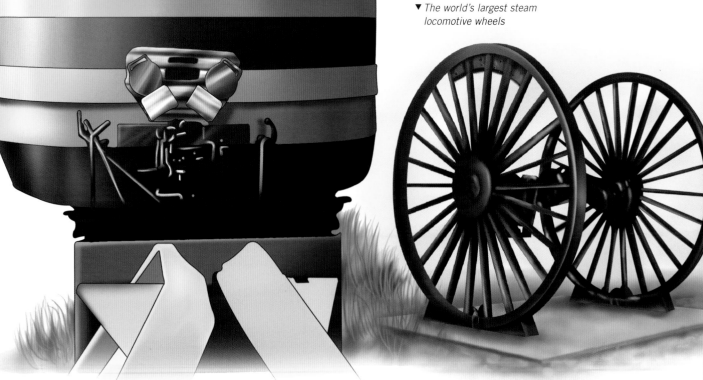

FACT FILE

- The National Railway Museum in York houses a vast array of railway timepieces, such as fob pocket watches and platform clocks. In the early 19th century, railway station staff were provided with fob watches to help them do their jobs on time.

- Earlier, men were specially hired to keep a lookout for approaching trains, to warn tracklayers. These "lookout" men blew their brass horns to warn workers to move away from the tracks. The horns are seen at many railway museums.

- The Fry Model Railway in Dublin, Ireland, is one of the world's largest miniature railway collections. Spread across 240 sq m (2, 583 sq ft), the exhibition shows handmade models of early and modern Irish trains.

What is the National Rail Museum in New Delhi famous for?

The National Railway Museum in India's capital city houses the oldest working, broad-gauge, steam locomotive, the *Fairy Queen*. It now runs as a luxury train in India, taking tourists on overnight trips to Rajasthan's Sariska Tiger Reserve.

Which object, commonly found at railway museums, was used to make announcements at railway stations?

Many national railway museums display handbells, which were commonly used to announce arrivals and departures of trains.

What does the National Tramway Museum have to do with cricket?

Several tramways are known to have been put to other uses after they were removed from service. The Leicester *76 Tramcar*, which was used as a cricket pavilion, is housed in the National Tramway Museum. Visitors can sit on the tram's wooden seats, which still bear the scars of spiked cricket boots!

◄ Before loudspeakers and computerised sounds, handbells like this one announced train arrivals and departures

▲ Early 19th-century timepiece used by station staff members

► The National Tramway Museum houses several models of trams as well as historic journals, documents and books on related vehicles

Where can one rent a locomotive?

The Florida Gulf Coast Rail Museum allows a person above 18 years, with a valid driving license, to run a locomotive! The museum has instructors who teach you all the controls, let you run it, and even give you a certificate.

When was the Norwegian Railway Museum built?

The Norwegian Railway Museum was established in Hamar in 1896. It is one of the oldest railway museums in the world.